OFFICERS and SOLDIERS of

THE FRENCH HUS 1786-1804

GW00385559

From the «Ancien Regime» to the Empire

Volume one

André JOUINEAU
Jean-Marie MONGIN
translated from the French by Alan McKay

HISTOIRE & COLLECTIONS

THE KING'S HUSSARS

Just over a century separates the creation of the first Hussar unit and the beginning of this study.

Before looking at the uniforms, it is worth dwelling a little on the tormented development and history of the Hussar regiments, and the task is not easy thanks to the pragmatism of the aristocratic proprietor-colonels which is not to be overestimated.

A turbulent development

The first royal Hussars regiment was formed in Strasbourg in 1693, after the good behaviour of 'these Hungarian deserters' whom the Maréchal of Luxemburg used to give the rear of the enemy troops a hard time. Disbanded in 1697, the regiment was reformed four years later. It was offered by the Elector of Bavaria to Louis XIV and took the name of *Saint-Genies Hussars* in 1707, then that of *Rattky-Hussars* and finally *Linden* or *Lynden*.

In 1719, Count Bercheny raised a Hungarian Hussar regiment… in Turkey and offered it to the King of France.

At Strasbourg in 1734, Count Esterhazy organised a regiment called successively the *Esterhazy-Hussars*, *David-Hussars*, *Turpin-Hussars* and finally the *Chamborant Hussars* in 1761.

In 1742, for the first time all the regiments were greatly reorganised which not only increased the strength of each regiment, but enabled three new ones to be created: the *Beausobre-Hussars*, the *Raugrave-Hussars* and the *Polleretzky-Hussars*.

A seventh regiment was created in 1745 and properly took the name of its owner: the *Ferrari-Hussars*.

Once again, with the increase of each company's strength in 1756, the regiments were completely reorganised: the *Linden* was attached to the *Bercheny*, *Beausobre* to the *Turpin*, *Ferrari* to the *Polleretzky*, and the *Raugrave* became the *'Volunteers from Liege'*.

It was then that the Prince of Nassau brought a regiment of German hussars into the service of the King of France; they took the name of *Nassau-Hussars*.

In 1757, the *Polleretzky Hussars* were disbanded and transferred to the *Bercheny* and *Turpin Hussars*. In 1761, the *Chamborant Hussars* replaced the *Turpin Hussars*. In the same year, the 'Fischer Legion' was changed into the *Conflans Hussars*. In 1762, the *Bercheny*, *Chamborant* and *Nassau* were reorganised.

The *Esterhazy Hussars* were created in 1764

THE HUSSAR REGIMENT IN 1788

When on a war footing the Hussar regiment in theory comprised 899 men of whom 853 were mounted. In peacetime, there were 699 Hussars with 653 mounted.

The headquarters staff was made up of the following:
- 1 Colonel (*Mestre-de-camp*)
- 1 Lieutenant-Colonel
- 1 Major
- 1 Second-Major
- 1 Quartermaster-Paymaster
- 4 Standard-Bearers
- 1 Surgeon-Major
- 1 Chaplain
- 2 Adjudants
- 1 Master-Smith
- 1 Master-Saddler
- 1 Master-Armourer
- 2 Replacement Captains

There were four squadrons and each had two companies. A squadron was commanded by a Squadron Commander. Each squadron had a Standard-Bearer to whom an extra Lieutenant and a Second-Lieutenant had to be added.

The Company consisted of:
- 1 Captain (First Captain or Second Captain)
- 1 Lieutenant
- 1 Second-Lieutenant
- 1 *Maréchal des Logis Chef*
- 2 *Maréchals des Logis*
- 4 Brigadiers
- 4 *«Appointés»*
- 1 Trumpeter
- 92 Hussars (67 in peacetime), 4 not mounted
- 1 child of the regiment

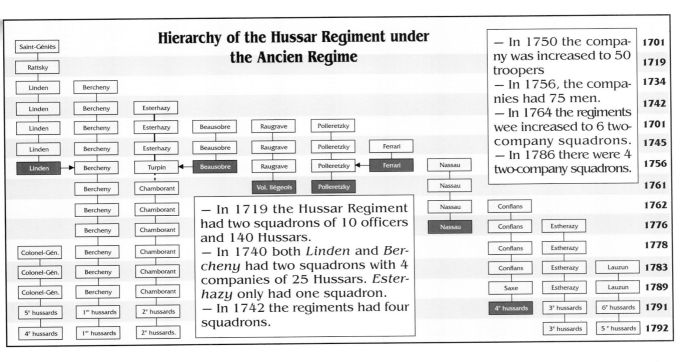

Hierarchy of the Hussar Regiment under the Ancien Regime

Saint-Géniès											**1701**
Rattsky											**1719**
Linden	Bercheny										**1734**
Linden	Bercheny	Esterhazy									**1742**
Linden	Bercheny	Esterhazy	Beausobre	Raugrave	Polleretzky						**1701**
Linden	Bercheny	Esterhazy	Beausobre	Raugrave	Polleretzky	Ferrari					**1745**
Linden	Bercheny	Turpin	Beausobre	Raugrave	Polleretzky	Ferrari	Nassau				**1756**
	Bercheny	Chamborant		Vol. liégeois	Polleretzky		Nassau				**1761**
	Bercheny	Chamborant					Nassau	Conflans			**1762**
	Bercheny	Chamborant					Nassau	Conflans	Estherazy		**1776**
	Bercheny	Chamborant						Conflans	Estherazy		**1778**
Colonel-Gén.	Bercheny	Chamborant						Conflans	Estherazy	Lauzun	**1783**
Colonel-Gén.	Bercheny	Chamborant						Saxe	Estherazy	Lauzun	**1789**
Colonel-Gén.	Bercheny	Chamborant						4e hussards	3e hussards	6e hussards	**1791**
5e hussards	1er hussards	2e hussards							3e hussards	5 e hussards	**1792**
4e hussards	1er hussards	2e hussards.									

— In 1750 the company was increased to 50 troopers
— In 1756, the companies had 75 men.
— In 1764 the regiments wee increased to 6 two-company squadrons.
— In 1786 there were 4 two-company squadrons.

— In 1719 the Hussar Regiment had two squadrons of 10 officers and 140 Hussars.
— In 1740 both *Linden* and *Bercheny* had two squadrons with 4 companies of 25 Hussars. *Esterhazy* only had one squadron.
— In 1742 the regiments had four squadrons.

and the Hussar arm reached a strength of 6 regiments. In 1776 the *Nassau Hussars* were disbanded.

In 1778 and 1779, the charge of *Colonel-General* of the Hussars was created for the Duke of Chartres and a *Colonel-General* Regiment was created which became number one in the Hussar arm. Its squadrons were formed by taking one squadron from each of the regiments already in existence.

In 1783, *'Lauzun's Volunteer Legion'* who had returned from its American campaign covered in glory became the *Lauzun Hussars*.

In 1789, the *Conflans Hussars* became the *Saxony Hussars*. In 1791 the Hussars regiments, like all the regiments of all the arms in the former Royal Army, lost their names and were given numbers, as follows: *Bercheny Hussars* became the 1st Hussar Regiment; *Chamborant Hussars* the 2nd; the *Saxony Hussars* (ex-*Conflans*) the 3rd; *Esterhazy Hussars* the 4th; the *Colonel-General* the 5th and *Lauzun's Hussars* the 6th.

In 1792, the *Saxony Hussars*, or rather the 4th Hussar Regiment turned traitor and went over, lock stock and barrel, into the Émigré camp; so

the *Colonel-General* Regiment became the 4th and the *Lauzun Regiment* became the 5th.

During the Ancien Régime, the Hussars were given the security and protection tasks, away from the battle and after it. The influence and success in this 'Little War' earned by the Ancien Régime's light troops, from which several Hussar regiments were created during the 18th century, gradually changed the role and the tasks of the Hussars, leading them progressively to the reconnoitering, harassment, pursuit and rapid intervention roles, indeed everything which eventually became the Hussars' 'little war' during the Empire.

The 1786 Regulations

On 1 October 1786, new regulations were brought out concerning uniforms, equipment and weapons for the King of France's Armies. To a greater or lesser degree, these regulations — in many ways they were almost legendary — set the standard for soldiers' uniforms to come until the middle of the First Empire. This was the beginning of the French-style uniform. Being a new and already prestigious arm the Hussars naturally had texts in the regulations for the cavalry which were applicable only to them. Basically these were as follows.

The Hussars wore Hungarian-style clothes: pelisse, dolman and breeches.

The **pelisse** was decorated on the front with 36 ornaments, made of square thread or woollen braids, 18 on each side.

In the middle, on the edge of the right side, there was a row of large round buttons and on each side there was another row of ball buttons. The braid went across from one row of buttons to the other. Those on the left made a row of 18 buttonholes on the edge. The lining was made of white sheepskin with black sheepskin for the border. On the collar there was a large cord with an olive-shaped button the same colour as the decorations, which was used to hold the pelisse in place without being worn.

There was no more precise description of the pelisse before 1812.

The **dolman** was shorter than the pelisse, had

the same number of buttons and the same decorations. Its lining was made of cloth and the bottom inside edge was covered with red skin. The narrow sleeves were made in a single piece... The opening at the cuff fastened with small hooks. The bottom of the sleeve was folded back over to reveal the lining, which formed a right-angled facing.

The breeches were Hungarian-style. The openings, the top and the rear stitching were decorated with flat braid. The breeches had a small fly. The braid on the side seams rose almost to the top of the thighs where it bent backwards and joined the small of the back.

The rest of the uniform was made up of a **waistcoat** and an **overcoat**, like those worn by the rest of the cavalry; a belt later called a scarf and then finally a **barrel-sash**, which was made up of a large crimson woollen rope with buttons the same colour as the decorations.

The **cap** or Hungarian-style shako was made of black felt lined with woollen cloth the same colour as the distinctive and bordered with a stripe. The pennant was worn either wrapped round the shako or simply unfurled.

The **forage cap** had a cord and knot and respected the same dispositions as the rest of the French Cavalry. The **coat** was made of green-coloured cloth for all the regiments except, so it would seem, for that of the Colonel-General which was blue. It had a hood but no facings.

The **boots** were made of blackened calf leather, cut in the Hungarian manner with spurs attached to the heels which were iron-tipped.

The **belt** was also Hungarian, made of white buffalo skin. Its four parts were joined by three copper rings. It was fastened with an S-shaped hook. The leather sword slings had copper buckles. The **sabretache** was borne by three leather slings which were adjusted

On the three rings of the belt. The two slings of the sabre were attached to the rings at the extremities (see page 15 for details).

The sabretache was originally a bag and was made of scarlet cloth held by a leather strap at the edge of the cloth. It was decorated with the King's monogramme (in this case Louis XVI) com-

THE HUSSAR'S LITTLE EQUIPMENT IN 1786

Clothes and accessories
— 3 shirts
— 2 black dimity collars
— 2 buckskin breeches
— 2 pairs of stockings
— 1 pair of shoes
— 1 pair of black gaiters
— 2 pairs of boot gaiters
— 2 handkerchiefs
— 1 collar buckle
— 1 pair of shoe buckles
— 2 pairs of garter buckles

Small articles
— 1 pair of scissors
— 1 wadding line
— 1 screwdriver
— 1 powder bag
— 1 brush

— 1 comb
— 1 cleaning comb
— 1 coat and hat brush
  Boot and shoe brushes
— 1 grease box for the copper items
— 1 brush for whitening the leatherwork
— 1 sewing dice thread, needles
— 1 button pull
— 1 needle

For brushing down the horse
— 1 brush
— 1 currycomb
— 1 sponge
— 1 comb
— 1 duster

This list of items applied to all cavalry and Dragoon units. The black dimity collar was issued to Hussars only.

Regiments	Pelisse	Dolman	Overcoat	Waistcoat	Facings	Breeches	Braid	Coat	Buttons	Shako	Cord
Col.-General	Scarlet	Royal blue	Royal blue	Royal blue	Scarlet	Royal blue	Yellow	Royal blue	Yellow	Scarlet	Yellow
Bercheny	Half-Royal blue	H-R blue	H-R blue	H-R blue	Garance	H-R blue	White	Green	White	Red	White
Chamborant	Brown	Brown	Brown	Brown	Garance	H-R blue	White	Green	White	H-R blue	White
Conflans	Green	Green	Green	Green	Garance	Garance	Yellow	Green	Yellow	Green	White
Estherazy	Silvery grey	Silvery grey	Silvery grey	Silvery grey	Garance	Silvery grey	Red	Green	White	White	Red
Lauzun	White	H-R blue	H-R blue	H-R blue	White	H-R blue	Lemon	Green	Yellow	H-R blue	White

prising large flat twisted braid also called a cordonnet and bordered with a stripe. The bottom was punched in bracket.

The rest of the equipment comprised a **shoulder belt** for the musket called 'bandoulière' in the regulations and made of white buffalo skin. It had an iron ring for the musket and a buckle and brass ring. It ended with a scalloped copper plate. The **cartridge case** was curved and made of black calf-skin.

The **shoulder-belt** for the case was made of white buffalo-skin. It was fixed to the case with two copper rings. Its left part had a copper buckle with a tongue to take the other half which had a scalloped copper plate.

The **portmanteau** was made of knitted wool the same colour as the distinctive of each article. The ends were rounded, surrounded with braid and with the same braid crossed over in the middle. It was opened thanks to five big knitted buttons.

All the Hussars, from the simple trooper to the officer commanding the regiment, had a **sabre** and a **pair of pistols**. The Brigadiers, «Appointés» and Hussars were also equipped with a musket. The officer's sabre had golden copper decorations.

The harnessing was naturally «à la Hongroise». The **shabrack** was made of sheep-skin bordered with woollen scallops the same colour as the distinctive. A woollen blanket completed the whole.

For the officers, the various ornaments, studs, etc., were forbidden. The shabrack was made of panther or tiger-skin bordered with cloth scallops the same colour as the distinctive. A silvery stripe was sewn over these scallops.

The trumpeters wore the livery of the *Mestre de Camp*. They wore a French coat and the cavalry jacket. The **coats** were edged with braid in front and decorated on each side in front on the neck on a level with the pocket, with six braid frogs. The sleeves were decorated with braid from one seam to the other. They wore skin breeches and the same boots and hat as the cavalry.

Only the trumpeters in the *Colonel-General Regiment* wore the Hungarian-style livery of the Duke of Chartres.

Officer's dress differed from the ordinary trooper's mainly in the quality of the cloth, the buttons which were silver or gold, and the braid which was either silver or gold depending on the distinctives. The **belt** was made of scarlet goat hair and the border of the pelisses was no longer made of sheepskin but fox throat fur.

Each regiment had distinctive colours; some arrangements and our plates will show the principal features of these items.

The table below summarises the way the distinctive colours for the six Hussar regiments concerned by the 1786 Regulations were distributed. Once again, the plates give the details of the various features.

As can be seen, except for the number of buttons and the rows of decorations (the plaits), or the size of the pelisse and the dolman which were shortened according to the fashion of the day, the basic silhouette of the French Hussar was now fixed for the next fifty years.

The long evolution of the 1786 Regulations enables the differences and the changes which were implemented during the different regimes to be shown.

Navy Volunteers, Lauzun's Legion

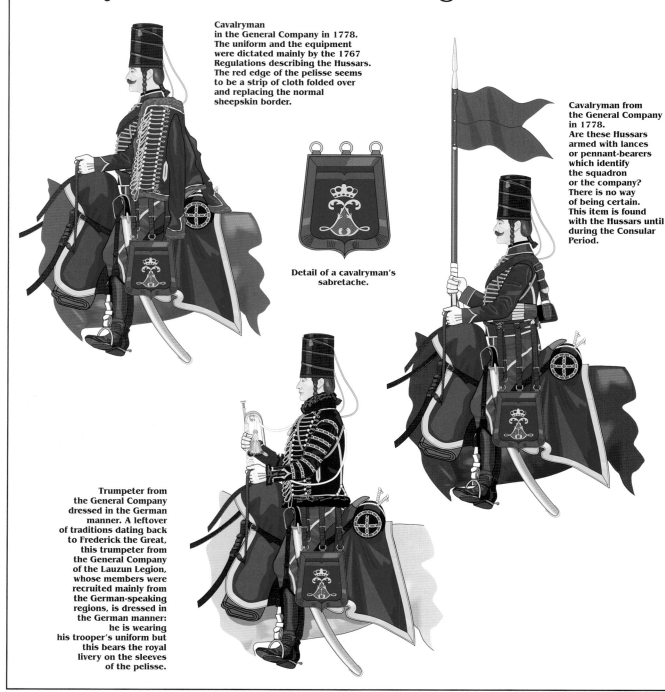

Cavalryman
in the General Company in 1778.
The uniform and the equipment
were dictated mainly by the 1767
Regulations describing the Hussars.
The red edge of the pelisse seems
to be a strip of cloth folded over
and replacing the normal
sheepskin border.

**Detail of a cavalryman's
sabretache.**

**Cavalryman from
the General Company
in 1778.**
Are these Hussars
armed with lances
or pennant-bearers
which identify
the squadron
or the company?
There is no way
of being certain.
This item is found
with the Hussars until
during the Consular
Period.

**Trumpeter from
the General Company
dressed in the German
manner.** A leftover
of traditions dating back
to Frederick the Great,
this trumpeter from
the General Company
of the Lauzun Legion,
whose members were
recruited mainly from
the German-speaking
regions, is dressed in
the German manner:
he is wearing
his trooper's uniform but
this bears the royal
livery on the sleeves
of the pelisse.

Navy Volunteers, Lauzun's Legion

Detail of an officer's sabretache.

Cavalryman from the Ordinary Company: He is wearing the same uniform as the General Company, but it is different in that the breeches and the edges of the pelisse are yellow.

Officer wearing full dress: in theory, the uniform is identical to that of the troopers, but a lot of liberties were taken. The felt cap was replaced by a fox-skin colback. The white pelisse, edged with fox-skin may have been sky-blue, like that of the troopers.

Trumpeter in the Ordinary Company wearing a coat à la Française: Unlike the preceding Trumpeter, he is wearing royal livery: a coat striped with crimson ribbon embellished with chain-stitched silver thread. This was regulation dress for trumpeters in the French Cavalry.

The 1786 Regulations

Colonel-General

Distinctive colours:
Royal blue and scarlet.
The braid on the dolman
and the pelisse
are bright yellow,
as are the stripes.

Bercheny

Distinctive colours:
Half-Royal blue
and scarlet.
All the trimmings are
white.

Chamborant

Distinctive colours:
Brown and sky blue.
The braid and the stripes
are silver for the officers.

Conflans

Distinctive
colours:
Light green
and scarlet.

Esterhazy

Distinctive
colours:
Silvery grey
and red.

Lauzun

Distinctive
colours:
Sky blue
and white.

The 1786 Regulations

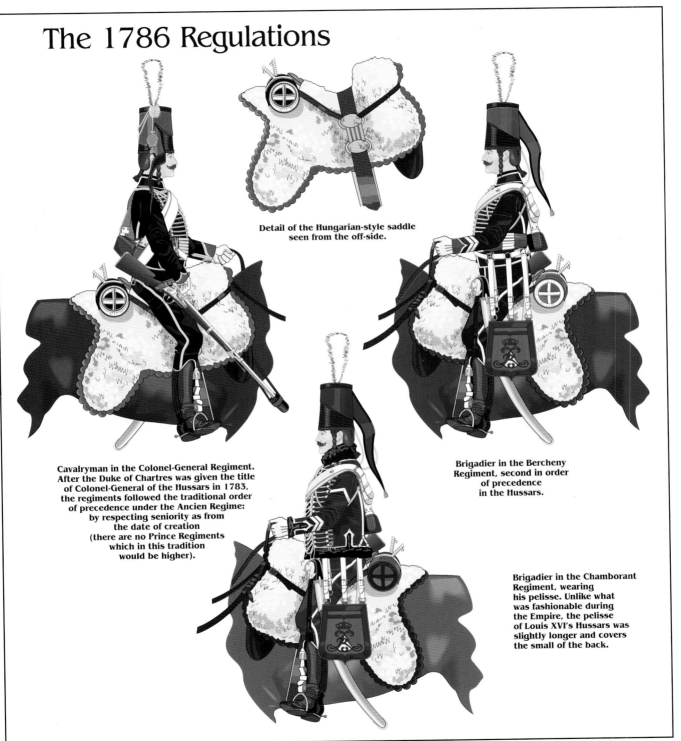

Detail of the Hungarian-style saddle
seen from the off-side.

Cavalryman in the Colonel-General Regiment.
After the Duke of Chartres was given the title
of Colonel-General of the Hussars in 1783,
the regiments followed the traditional order
of precedence under the Ancien Regime:
by respecting seniority as from
the date of creation
(there are no Prince Regiments
which in this tradition
would be higher).

Brigadier in the Bercheny
Regiment, second in order
of precedence
in the Hussars.

Brigadier in the Chamborant
Regiment, wearing
his pelisse. Unlike what
was fashionable during
the Empire, the pelisse
of Louis XVI's Hussars was
slightly longer and covers
the small of the back.

The 1786 Regulations

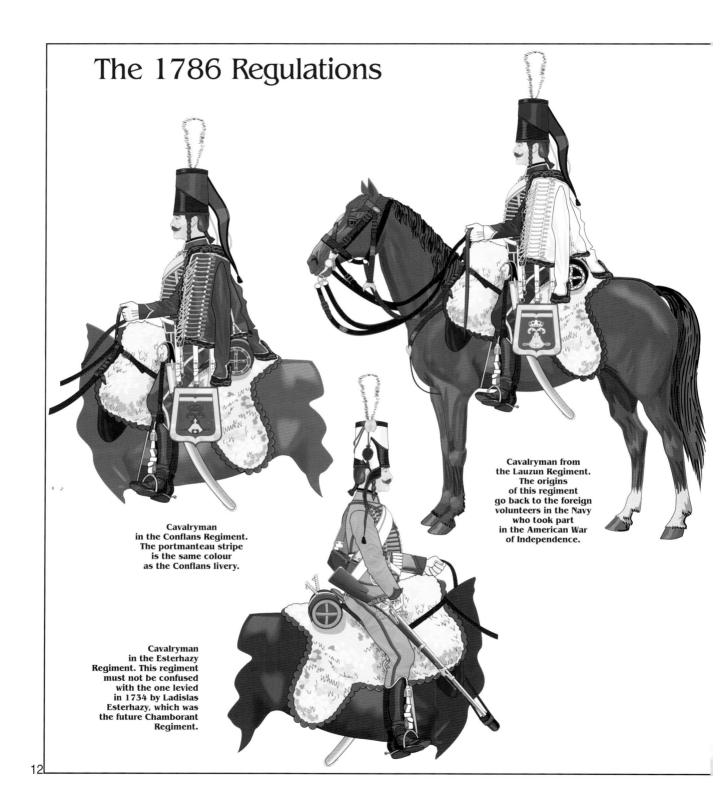

Cavalryman
in the Conflans Regiment.
The portmanteau stripe
is the same colour
as the Conflans livery.

Cavalryman from
the Lauzun Regiment.
The origins
of this regiment
go back to the foreign
volunteers in the Navy
who took part
in the American War
of Independence.

Cavalryman
in the Esterhazy
Regiment. This regiment
must not be confused
with the one levied
in 1734 by Ladislas
Esterhazy, which was
the future Chamborant
Regiment.

The 1786 Regulations

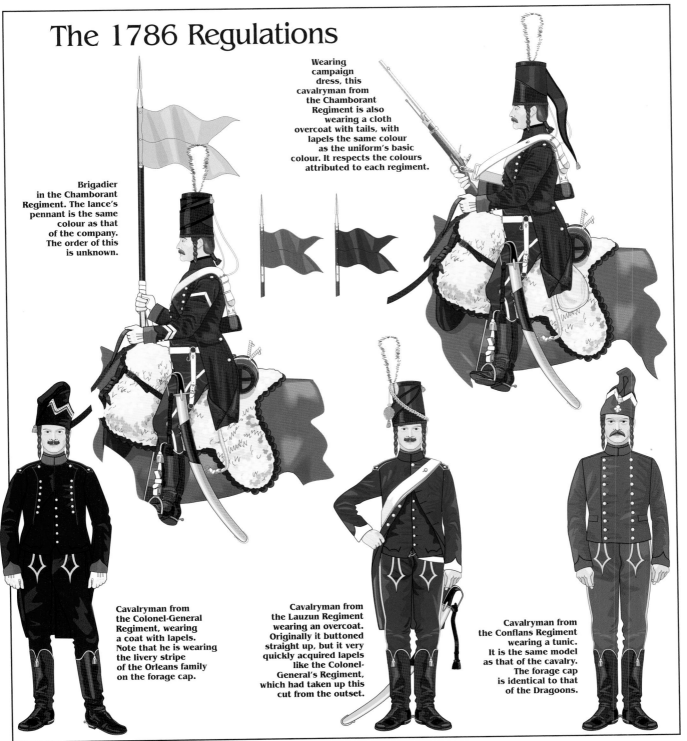

Wearing campaign dress, this cavalryman from the Chamborant Regiment is also wearing a cloth overcoat with tails, with lapels the same colour as the uniform's basic colour. It respects the colours attributed to each regiment.

Brigadier in the Chamborant Regiment. The lance's pennant is the same colour as that of the company. The order of this is unknown.

Cavalryman from the Colonel-General Regiment, wearing a coat with lapels. Note that he is wearing the livery stripe of the Orleans family on the forage cap.

Cavalryman from the Lauzun Regiment wearing an overcoat. Originally it buttoned straight up, but it very quickly acquired lapels like the Colonel-General's Regiment, which had taken up this cut from the outset.

Cavalryman from the Conflans Regiment wearing a tunic. It is the same model as that of the cavalry. The forage cap is identical to that of the Dragoons.

Items of Clothing

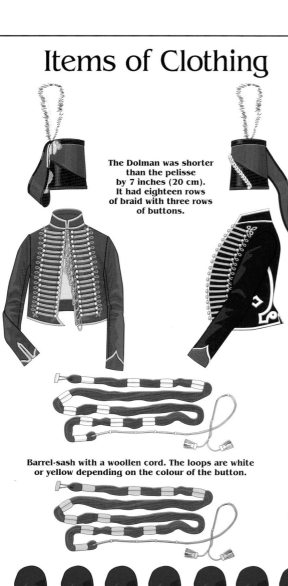

The Dolman was shorter than the pelisse by 7 inches (20 cm). It had eighteen rows of braid with three rows of buttons.

Barrel-sash with a woollen cord. The loops are white or yellow depending on the colour of the button.

Felt hat with a long pennon which could be furled around the body of the hat. This 'Mirliton' was in the form of a flattened cone, about 30 cm (12 in). A cord attached to the hat and having two flounders was used for keeping the hat on the man's head, being tied around the man's chest. When not used the cord was plaited on the front of the hat.

Hungarian-style breeches. They have a fly flap, embellished with almost diamond-shaped stripes: the stripes are also on the side seams. The bottoms of the breeches fasten by means of 10 hooks and a strap under the arch of the foot, all to hold them in place.

The pelisse bears 36 buttonholes, eighteen on each side with as many spherical buttons to do it up with. 36 half-spherical buttons are attached to the end of each plait. The lining is made of white sheepskin edged with black sheepskin.

Rank stripes for troopers and lower NCOs.

1. Re-enlisted.

2. Furrier.

3. *Appointé*.

4. Brigadier.

5. *Maréchal des Logis* with the gold variant depending on the colour of the button.

6. *Maréchal des Logis chef*.

7. Adjudant (NCO).

1   2   3   4   5   6   7

Coat with lapels, French-cut. This item of clothing was the most worn by the Hussars, on duty or on campaign.

Tail coat buttoning up straight attributed to the Esterhazy Hussars.

14

Weapons and Equipment

Model 1776 Sabre.
Apart from the three models shown
here, there were many others.
These can be discovered by reading
the book by Michel Pétard on swords
and knives.

Hungarian-style belt made of white buffalo hide, equipped
with the two slings which enable the sabre to be held up,
and the three sabretache slings.

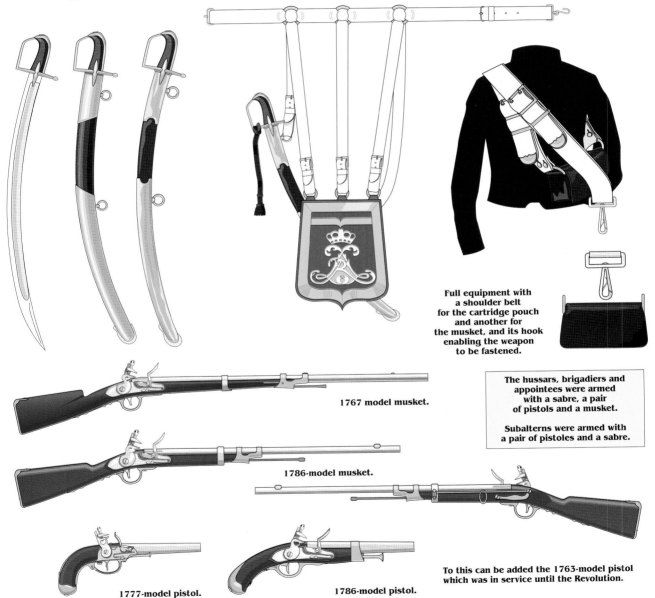

Full equipment with
a shoulder belt
for the cartridge pouch
and another for
the musket, and its hook
enabling the weapon
to be fastened.

1767 model musket.

1786-model musket.

The hussars, brigadiers and
appointees were armed
with a sabre, a pair
of pistols and a musket.

Subalterns were armed with
a pair of pistoles and a sabre.

1777-model pistol.

1786-model pistol.

To this can be added the 1763-model pistol
which was in service until the Revolution.

Harnesses, etc.

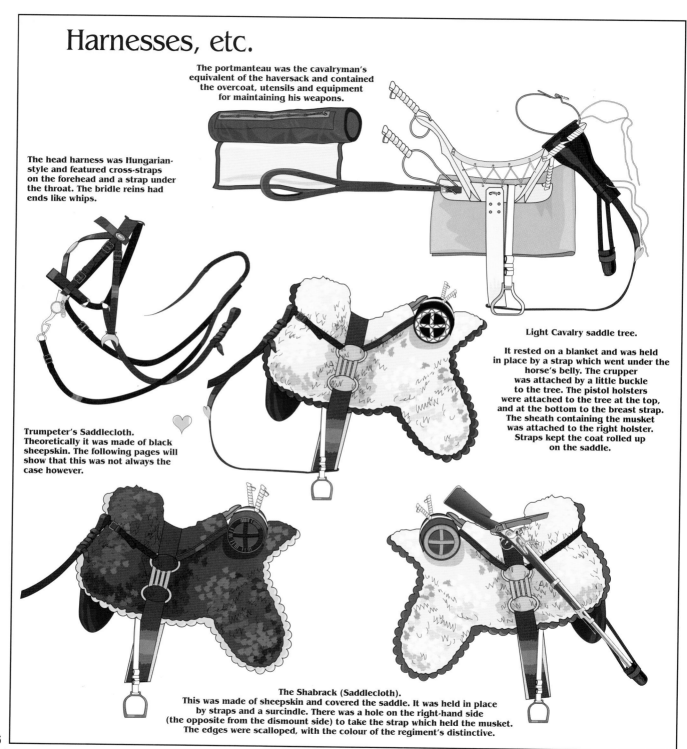

The portmanteau was the cavalryman's equivalent of the haversack and contained the overcoat, utensils and equipment for maintaining his weapons.

The head harness was Hungarian-style and featured cross-straps on the forehead and a strap under the throat. The bridle reins had ends like whips.

Light Cavalry saddle tree.

It rested on a blanket and was held in place by a strap which went under the horse's belly. The crupper was attached by a little buckle to the tree. The pistol holsters were attached to the tree at the top, and at the bottom to the breast strap. The sheath containing the musket was attached to the right holster. Straps kept the coat rolled up on the saddle.

Trumpeter's Saddlecloth. Theoretically it was made of black sheepskin. The following pages will show that this was not always the case however.

The Shabrack (Saddlecloth).
This was made of sheepskin and covered the saddle. It was held in place by straps and a surcindle. There was a hole on the right-hand side (the opposite from the dismount side) to take the strap which held the musket. The edges were scalloped, with the colour of the regiment's distinctive.

The Trumpeters

Trumpeters from the Colonel-General Regiment.

On the left wearing German-style dress: pelisse with 7 stripes on the sleeves in the livery of the Orléans family. The cord of the trumpet is tricolour; the pennant of the trumpet also bears the arms of the Orléans family. On the right, the trumpeter is wearing an overcoat. We think that the coat had no pockets; at most the turnbacks were pinned up and perhaps decorated with a Fleur de Lys.

Trumpeter from the Chamborant Regiment.

Strangely enough, this trumpeter is not at all wearing any of his regiment's colours. Perhaps the Mestre de camp wanted to give his regiment a bit more colour. This drawing appeared in a special edition of the Sabretache devoted to the Hussars. It was itself inspired by a drawing by General Vanson, the first director to the Musée de l'Armée. The French-style coat is decorated with the stripe of the Chamborant livery. Two false sleeves have been sewn on the man's back; they start from the shoulder seam and button onto the waist buttons. The trumpet shoulder belt with a silver fringe was probably decorated with the arms of France.

The Trumpeters

Trumpeter from the Conflans Hussars.

The coat is French-style with its specific livery stripe. The false sleeves were attached in the same way as the Chamborant trumpeter.

Trumpeter from the Saxony Hussars.

In 1789, the Conflans Regiment became Saxon and changed owners. The troopers' uniform remained unchanged. On the other hand the trumpeters probably changed their coat as well as their livery stripe as shown below.

Lauzun Hussars Trumpeter.

This is another example of a trumpeter's coat which scarcely respects the regiment's colours except for the turnbacks and the facings. Most of the trumpeters wore skin trousers unlike the Hungarian-style trousers of the rest of the troopers. It is probable that they wore knee-length boots, then gave them up in favour of Hungarian boots.

The officers

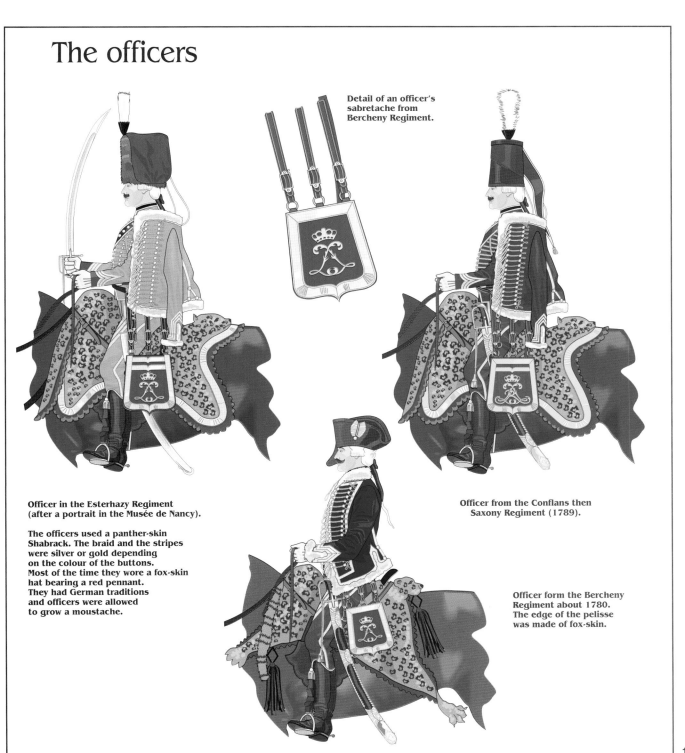

Detail of an officer's sabretache from Bercheny Regiment.

Officer in the Esterhazy Regiment (after a portrait in the Musée de Nancy).

The officers used a panther-skin Shabrack. The braid and the stripes were silver or gold depending on the colour of the buttons. Most of the time they wore a fox-skin hat bearing a red pennant. They had German traditions and officers were allowed to grow a moustache.

Officer from the Conflans then Saxony Regiment (1789).

Officer form the Bercheny Regiment about 1780. The edge of the pelisse was made of fox-skin.

Officers' Marks of Rank

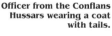

Officer from the Conflans Hussars about 1788 wearing a coat with tails.

Like the troopers, the officers wore a coat with tails cut in the French style with the pointed facings and lapels of the Light Cavalry. Rank is shown by the epaulettes which were identical throughout all the corps according to the 1786 regulations. There was a custom in the light cavalry whereby the junior officers only wore a single epaulette; this was non-regulation.

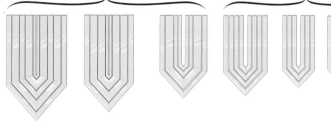

1 2 3 4 5 6 7

Officer from the Conflans Hussars wearing a coat with tails.

The coats worn for the service dress were of the same colour as the regiment. The officers could replace their sabre with a sword.

Officers' marks of rank *(from left to right)*.

1. Mestre de camp (colonel).

2. Lieutenant-Colonel.

3. Major (the senior officers had two flat braid plaits on the seams of their breeches, on the back of the dolman and the pelisse).

4. Capitaine-Commandant.

5. Capitaine en second.

6. Lieutenant.

7. Sub-Lieutenant and Standard-Bearer (the standard-bearer had one stripe like the Sub-Lieutenant and the epaulette with a red fringe and body with a golden edge).

Standards

The standard of the Colonel Company
of the Colonel-General Regiment
bearing the Orléans arms.

The standard of the Lauzun Legion
during the American War
of Independence.

A standard of an ordinary company
in the Colonel-General Regiment
with the Orléans arms.

The standard of an ordinary company
in the Lauzun Regiment bearing
the Lauzun arms on the obverse.

We have consulted Pierre Charrié, a
specialist in French Army standards
and who described Hussar standards
for this period in the special issue of
Sabretache devoted to the Hussars
of the 1735-1815 period, and in his
book on the standards and flags of
the King. There are no illustrations of
these flags but there are brief
descriptions which enable us to
present this model while we wait for
further discoveries which will enable
us to reconstitute these standards
which were destroyed during the
Revolution.

Hussars during the Constitutional Monarchy

According to the regulations of 1791, the whole of the cavalry did not change uniforms except for certain small details like replacing the white cockade with a tricolour one, removing the livery stripes, officers wearing their hats like the troopers, the names of the proprietor Colonels being abolished and replaced by a number corresponding to their seniority, etc.

Appointé in the 1st Hussars (formerly Bercheny).

Officer in the 1st Hussars (formerly Bercheny).

Cavalryman in the 2nd Hussars (formerly Chamborant).

Maréchal des Logis **in the 3rd Hussars (formerly Esterhazy).**

Cavalryman in the 4th Hussars (formerly Saxony).

Hussars, 1790-1792

Officer in the 4th Hussars (formerly Saxony) wearing an overcoat.

Trumpeter in the 6th Hussars (formerly Lauzun). Following the removal of the stripes the colours of the proprietor colonels, the trumpeters adopted the royal blue French-style coat, with the livery stripe, and were distinguished by the colour of the facings and the buttons.

Cavalryman from the 6th Hussars (formerly Lauzun).

Cavalryman of the 5th Hussars (formerly Colonel-General) in full dress and (left) wearing an overcoat.

Cavalryman from the 5th Hussars wearing an overcoat (the former Colonel-General Regiment).

23

THE VOLUNTEER AND EMIGRE HUSSARS

The Volunteer Hussars had careers like their foster mother, the Revolution: sometimes glorious, sometimes laughable, but always chaotic.

The main units were created in 1792 at the time of the mass levies, during the great revolutionary and patriotic surges of enthusiasm.

These corps were often levied on the initiative of a commander and the recruiting and operating methods were not without recalling the despised methods of the Ancien Regime. The syndrome of the proprietor colonel was still around…

The New Corps of Volunteer Hussars

The Hussars — because of the reputation they had of being adventurous, sabre-wielding rebels very much in line with the new wind blowing across France — seemed to have encouraged enough vocations among the soon-to-be warlords of this still very young Republic. We propose going over these units with such evocative names very briefly.

The Cavalrymen of the *Moselle Legion* or *Kellermann's Legion* came from the squadrons of the former *Saxony Hussars* (the 4th Hussar Regiment of 1791) and the *Royal German* who remained faithful to the Republic. The creation of this corps went back to May 1792. The first three squadrons of the 4th Hussars were those who emigrated in May 1792.

In July 1792, the *Death's Head Hussars*, a squadron of Parisian volunteers, were created.

Two *Corps of Liberté Hussars* were raised by the law of 2 September 1792. The *1st Corps of Liberté Hussars* was raised in Paris by Citizen Ruttau. The *Second Corps* was levied in Lille by Citizen Dumont.

On 2 September of the same year, Citizen Boyer changed his 200 volunteers into *Défenseurs de la Liberté et de l'Egalité*. They became the 7th Hussars twenty days later.

The *German legion* was also created by decree, dated 4 September 1792. This corps was added to the new 24th Chasseurs à Cheval on 26 June 1793; it became the 11th Hussars on 28 July 1793, then the 29th Dragoons on 24 September 1803.

The decree of 22 September also authorised one Lamothe to raise a corps of volunteer light cavalry which immediately became the 8th Hussars for a few months.

Colonel Fabrefonds formed the *Fabrefonds Scouts* on 1 October 1792 in Nancy.

In the Nord, a month later Citizen Mairiaux created the *Jemmapes Hussars* or the *Black Hussars of the North*.

Four other Hussar corps were created before the end of 1792: the *Hainaut Hussars*, the *'Poacher' Hussars*, the *Ardennes Legion Hussars* and the *Egalité Hussars*.

At the end of 1792, the *Liberté Hussars* from Lille became the 8th Hussars too. In 1793, the *Death's Head Hussars*, the *Egalité Hussars* and a part of those from the *Alps Legion* raised the previous year were formed into the 14th Chasseur à Cheval regiment.

The *Fabrefonds Scouts* became the 9th Hussars in February 1793.

It is also worth mentioning the *Mountain Hussars*, raised in 1793 for the Army of the Western Pyrenees. They became the 12th Hussars before being transformed into the 30th Dragoon Regiment.

The *Partisan Corps of the Army* of the Rhine was formed on 7 October 1793 by General Leclerc de Landremont. On 25 August this corps was added to the 7 Bis Hussars.

In January 1795, the *Alps Hussars* were created (not to be confused with the *Alp Legion Hussars*) by amalgamating elements of the *Mountain Dragoons* and other units from the Vienne region. After a number of adventures they formed the short-lived 13th Hussars in September 1795.

As can be seen in the following pages, on the plates, the revolutionary or war-like symbolism was not restricted to the decoration of sabretaches and the corps all rivalled with each other in patriotic enthusiasm and revolutionary fervour.

But the volunteers for the very young Republic did not have the exclusive rights; the former aristocrats and émigrés also raised a large number of volunteers abroad. And even if only a few did not pass away into oblivion, in the same way they helped to form and perpetuate this light and independent spirit and the heroic attitudes so dear to the light cavalrymen.

The Emigré Hussars

The *Salm-Kirburg Hussar Corps* was raised in December 1791 by an agreement between the French

The *Death's Head Hussars* Squadron

The *Death's Head Hussars* Squadron was an example for more than one reason.

The squadron was made up of two companies under the orders of a **headquarters** staff which included:
— 1 Squadron Commander
— 1 Quarter-Master-Paymaster (*Maréchal des Logis*)
— 1 Adjudant (NCO)
— 1 Chaplain
— 1 Groom
— 1 Blacksmith
— 1 Master Tailor
— 1 Master Cobbler
— 1 Master Saddler

The **company** comprised:
— 1 Captain (First or Second Captain)
— 1 Lieutenant
— 1 Second-lieutenant
— 1 *Maréchal des Logis Chef*
— 4 *Maréchals des Logis*
— 1 *Brigadier* Furrier
— 8 *Brigadiers*
— 1 Trumpeter
— 105 Hussars

These were figures which the Volunteers from Paris, raised in June 1792, probably never attained; this has been demonstrated by Rigo who produced the rolls of the unit, showing that in April 1793 there were only 131 Hussars instead of the planned 210.

After a career which did not live up to the claims of the unit's symbolic reputation — Valmy remained the unit's one and only moment of glory, amid a series of moves, retreats and billets — the squadron, or what was left of it, was transferred to the very new 14th Regiment of Chasseurs à Cheval, with the four companies of the *Alps Legion Hussars* and the eight companies of the *Egalité Hussars* in April 1793.

Princes and the Prince of Salm-Kirburg, according to privileges granted to German Regiments in French service. They were integrated into Condé's Army, these Hussars fought on the Rhine, Holland and in Germany. They were dismissed at the end of 1795. Meanwhile, in spite of their engagement, they went into English service although they did not obey their new masters any more than they did their old ones.

The *Saxony Hussars*, the former 4th Hussar Regiment, kept their name even after their flight from France in May 1792. Like a lot of émigré units, the regiment went over into Austrian service.

The volunteers who made up the *Bercheny Hussars* emigrated in 1792. The regiment was incorporated into the Austrian Army and took part in the Dutch Campaign. In 1798 the regiment was reformed and incorporated into the Austrian 13th Light Dragoons.

In 1794, Etienne de Baschi, Count of Cayla, raised a cavalry corps, the *Baschi du Cayla Hussars*, at his own cost and recruited mainly from Alsatian émigrés. With Condé's Army, they fought on the Rhine and then in Bavaria before forming the kernel of the future Enghien Dragoons in 1798, in the service of Russia.

The *Damas Legion* Volunteers, after the name of the Count of Damas, a French officer who fought alongside the Stadthouder of Holland, were formed at the end of May 1793.

They included a squadron of Hussars. The legion fought in the north and went into Dutch service before joining the English; then it fought in Germany and ended up in Condé's Army, which was soon amalgamated into the Tsar's Army.

The *Rohan Hussars* comprising two regiments were raised by the Prince of Rohan, the first in March 1794 and the second in January 1795. The first fought in Holland with the English and mutinied before being sent to the West Indies. At the end of 1795, the two regiments were joined together and the new regiment set off in 1796 for the islands. It was disbanded in 1797.

The *Hompesh Hussars* were raised by Baron Charles Hompesh in February 1794. They ended their short career in October 1797 after being decimated in the West Indies.

The *Béon Legion Hussars* were created in order to serve in Holland in March 1793 and went over to the British at the beginning of 1795, they were disbanded in 1796.

The *York Hussar Regiment* was created in May 1793 among the Émigrés; it had British officers and took part in the Dutch Campaign; it was transferred to the West Indies where it was wiped out. It was disbanded in 1802.

The *Choiseul Hussars* were raised by the Duke of Choiseul-Stainville in March 1794.

The regiment did not have anything to do so it was disbanded in March 1796.

The Volunteer Hussars of the Republic

**Cavalryman from
the *1st Corps of 'Hussars de la Liberté'*.**

A decree from the National Assembly authorised
a 400-men strong corps of *'Hussards de la Liberté'*
('Liberty Hussars') to be formed.
It seemed more from economy that the cavalrymen
wore a French-style uniform rather than
a Hungarian one. Moreover the high command
suggested that the braid on the coat
be removed; this was approved higher up.
The Liberty Hussars therefore wore
a coat which buttoned straight up
until they were integrated into
the Hussars to form the 7th bis.

**Cavalryman from the *2nd Corps
of 'Hussars de la Liberté'*.**

They were distinguished from
the 1st Corps by the colour
of the buttons and the braid.
Commanded by Citizen Dumon,
he designated them as the
1st Hussars of the Republic,
then proclaimed them
the 8th Regiment even though
there already was a number 8.
Finally Dumouriez removed
Dumon from his command
and formed them into
an element of the 10th Hussars
on 25 March 1793.

**a *'Liberty Hussar'* during
the Dutch Campaign 1793-94.**

The source is a German drawing kept
in the Bibliothèque Nationale.
At the time, the volunteer hussars
were already in the 10th Hussars
whose distinctive colours are shown except
for the plaits and the buttons.

The Volunteer Hussars of the Republic

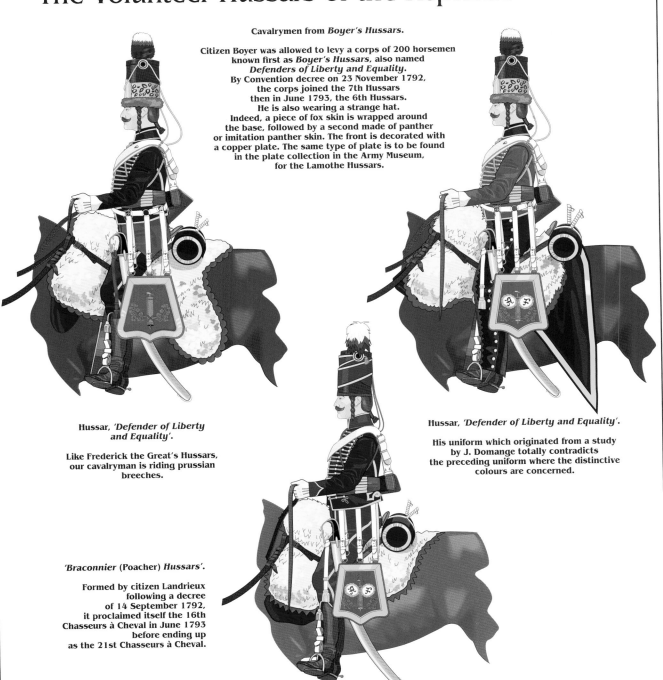

Cavalrymen from *Boyer's Hussars*.

Citizen Boyer was allowed to levy a corps of 200 horsemen
known first as *Boyer's Hussars*, also named
Defenders of Liberty and Equality.
By Convention decree on 23 November 1792,
the corps joined the 7th Hussars
then in June 1793, the 6th Hussars.
He is also wearing a strange hat.
Indeed, a piece of fox skin is wrapped around
the base, followed by a second made of panther
or imitation panther skin. The front is decorated with
a copper plate. The same type of plate is to be found
in the plate collection in the Army Museum,
for the Lamothe Hussars.

**Hussar, *'Defender of Liberty
and Equality'*.**

Like Frederick the Great's Hussars,
our cavalryman is riding prussian
breeches.

Hussar, *'Defender of Liberty and Equality'*.

His uniform which originated from a study
by J. Domange totally contradicts
the preceding uniform where the distinctive
colours are concerned.

'Braconnier (Poacher) *Hussars'*.

Formed by citizen Landrieux
following a decree
of 14 September 1792,
it proclaimed itself the 16th
Chasseurs à Cheval in June 1793
before ending up
as the 21st Chasseurs à Cheval.

The Volunteer Hussars of the Republic

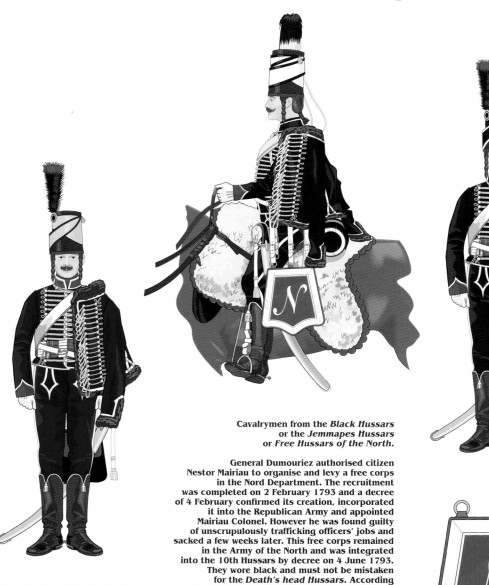

**Cavalrymen from the *Black Hussars*
or the *Jemmapes Hussars*
or *Free Hussars of the North*.**

General Dumouriez authorised citizen
Nestor Mairiau to organise and levy a free corps
in the Nord Department. The recruitment
was completed on 2 February 1793 and a decree
of 4 February confirmed its creation, incorporated
it into the Republican Army and appointed
Mairiau Colonel. However he was found guilty
of unscrupulously trafficking officers' jobs and
sacked a few weeks later. This free corps remained
in the Army of the North and was integrated
into the 10th Hussars by decree on 4 June 1793.
They wore black and must not be mistaken
for the *Death's head Hussars*. According
to the little pictorial and documentary evidence
we have and without being able to confirm it,
the dolman's facings were red, the plaits plain
white. The sabretache was decorated with
an 'N' according to other sources.

Fabrefond Scouts or Fabrefond Hussars.

Created by Colonel Fabrefond on 1 October
1792 for the Army of the Centre.
On 26 February 1793, this corps of volunteers
was integrated into the 9th Hussars
and then was moved to the Army
of the North to make up the 8th.

Hussar of the Alps

This corps was formed on 31 January 1793 by joining together the *Hussars of the Alps* (formerly the *Mountain Dragoons*), a surplus of horse scouts in the Army of the South and four companies from the cavalry depot in Vienne. On 1 September 1793 the *Hussars of the Alps* became the *Regiment of the Alps* and adopted the Number 13 in the Hussars although it did not last long, being disbanded at Lodi on 18 May 1796.

Our cavalryman opposite
is shown wearing
an overcoat. See Emile Fort's
collection preserved
at the Bibliothèque Nationale.

Hussars of the Alps, trumpeter
wearing an overcoat.

Death's Head Hussars

By a decree dated 12 June 1792, the Convention authorised the levying of a corps with two companies of Hussars. Like the others it did not last long. Joined to the *Equality Hussars*, they formed the 13th Chasseurs à Cheval, but the formation was delayed. They finally formed the 14th Chasseurs à Cheval.

In spite of its short existence and a strength of around 300 cavalrymen, this corps of Hussars fired the imagination of contemporaries and uniformologists so much, that it is the most represented of the Republic's hussar units.

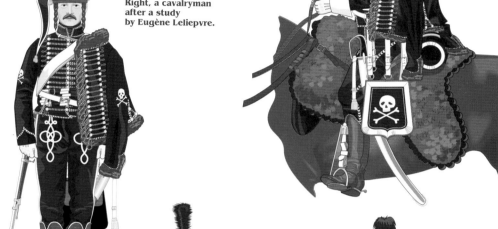

Cavalryman from the *Death's Head Hussars* after a drawing from the collection in the Dresden Museum and taken up by Rigo on his plate N° U3.

Right, a cavalryman after a study by Eugène Leliepvre.

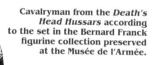

Cavalryman from the *Death's Head Hussars* according to the set in the Bernard Franck figurine collection preserved at the Musée de l'Armée.

Cavalryman from the *Death's Head Hussars* with different harness equipment.

Cavalryman from the *Death's Head Hussars*, after the Valmont collection preserved in the Bibliothèque Nationale and taken up by Rigo in his plate N° U3.

Death's Head Hussars

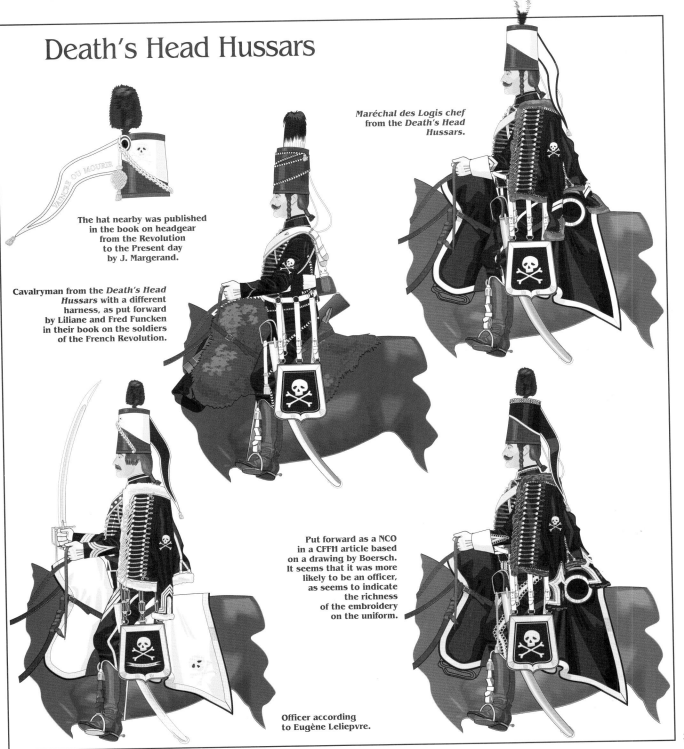

The hat nearby was published
in the book on headgear
from the Revolution
to the Present day
by J. Margerand.

Cavalryman from the *Death's Head Hussars* with a different harness, as put forward by Liliane and Fred Funcken in their book on the soldiers of the French Revolution.

Maréchal des Logis chef
from the *Death's Head
Hussars*.

Put forward as a NCO
in a CFFH article based
on a drawing by Boersch.
It seems that it was more
likely to be an officer,
as seems to indicate
the richness
of the embroidery
on the uniform.

Officer according
to Eugène Leliepvre.

31

The Mountain Hussars

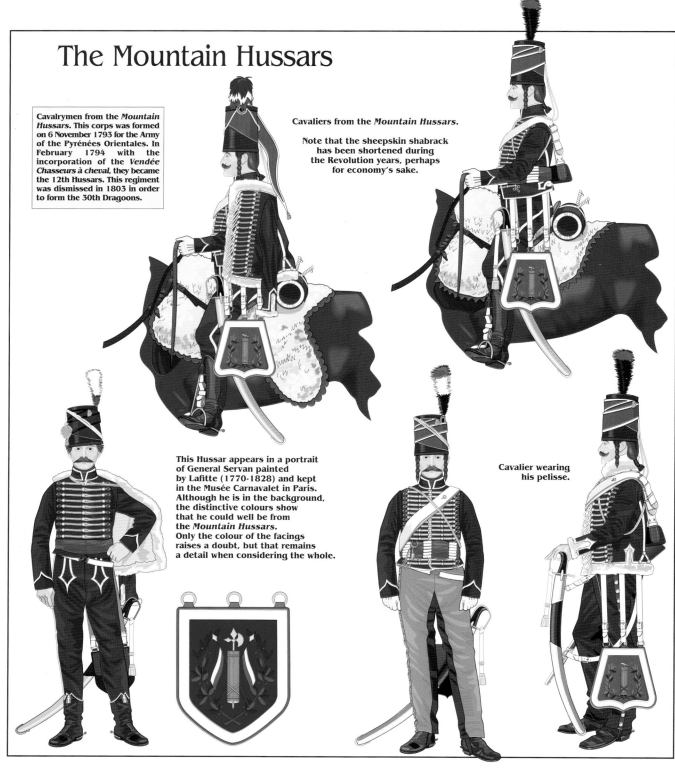

Cavalrymen from the *Mountain Hussars*. This corps was formed on 6 November 1793 for the Army of the Pyrénées Orientales. In February 1794 with the incorporation of the *Vendée Chasseurs à cheval*, they became the 12th Hussars. This regiment was dismissed in 1803 in order to form the 30th Dragoons.

Cavaliers from the *Mountain Hussars*.

Note that the sheepskin shabrack has been shortened during the Revolution years, perhaps for economy's sake.

This Hussar appears in a portrait of General Servan painted by Lafitte (1770-1828) and kept in the Musée Carnavalet in Paris. Although he is in the background, the distinctive colours show that he could well be from the *Mountain Hussars*. Only the colour of the facings raises a doubt, but that remains a detail when considering the whole.

Cavalier wearing his pelisse.

The Hussars of the Damas legion

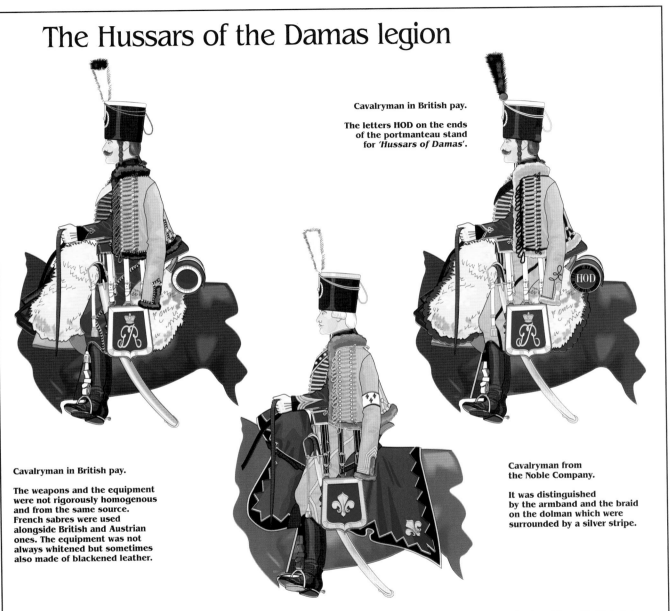

Cavalryman in British pay.

The letters HOD on the ends
of the portmanteau stand
for *'Hussars of Damas'*.

Cavalryman in British pay.

The weapons and the equipment
were not rigorously homogenous
and from the same source.
French sabres were used
alongside British and Austrian
ones. The equipment was not
always whitened but sometimes
also made of blackened leather.

**Cavalryman from
the Noble Company.**

It was distinguished
by the armband and the braid
on the dolman which were
surrounded by a silver stripe.

Count Etienne-Charles de Damas-Cruz, chief of staff of the Émigré corps during the siege of Maastricht in February 1793, asked the Stathouder for permission to organise a legion of French *émigrés*. The Dutch prince answered favourably which was then put to Monsieur the Regent of France, the Duke of Berry, future King Louis XVIII. The legion was formed at the end of May 1793. The corps comprised some infantry (two battalions) and a squadron of Hussars created a few months later. The Legion fought in Belgium and in the north of France. In 1793, it left Dutch service to join the British and then defended the banks of the Rhine against the Army of General Moreau.

In 1796, the Legion was practically dismissed from His Majesty's service and kept in reserve. After all sorts of incidents with the British administration, and the situation in Holland, the corps joined the Army of Condé and fought in Bavaria and then returned to the banks of the Rhine. In January 1797, the hussars numbered about 400 men including the officers, and the combat train (horses, wagons, pack mules and drivers).

In September 1797, Condé's army went into Russian service and in January 1798, the corps was dismissed and amalgamated with the other groups of Hussars to form the Enghien Dragoons.

The Hussars with the Émigré Troops

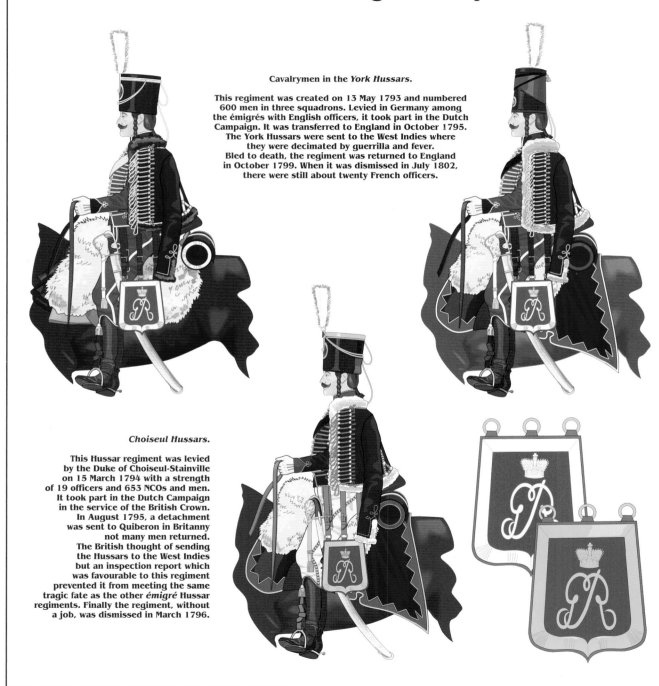

Cavalrymen in the *York Hussars*.

This regiment was created on 13 May 1793 and numbered 600 men in three squadrons. Levied in Germany among the émigrés with English officers, it took part in the Dutch Campaign. It was transferred to England in October 1795. The York Hussars were sent to the West Indies where they were decimated by guerrilla and fever. Bled to death, the regiment was returned to England in October 1799. When it was dismissed in July 1802, there were still about twenty French officers.

***Choiseul Hussars*.**

This Hussar regiment was levied by the Duke of Choiseul-Stainville on 15 March 1794 with a strength of 19 officers and 653 NCOs and men. It took part in the Dutch Campaign in the service of the British Crown. In August 1795, a detachment was sent to Quiberon in Britanny not many men returned. The British thought of sending the Hussars to the West Indies but an inspection report which was favourable to this regiment prevented it from meeting the same tragic fate as the other *émigré* Hussar regiments. Finally the regiment, without a job, was dismissed in March 1796.

The Hussars with the Émigré Troops

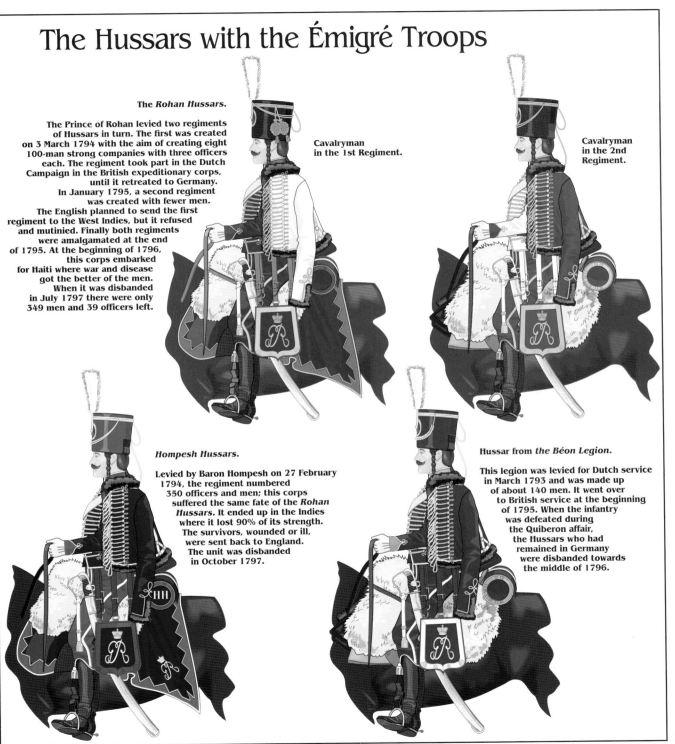

The *Rohan Hussars*.

The Prince of Rohan levied two regiments of Hussars in turn. The first was created on 3 March 1794 with the aim of creating eight 100-man strong companies with three officers each. The regiment took part in the Dutch Campaign in the British expeditionary corps, until it retreated to Germany.
In January 1795, a second regiment was created with fewer men.
The English planned to send the first regiment to the West Indies, but it refused and mutinied. Finally both regiments were amalgamated at the end of 1795. At the beginning of 1796, this corps embarked for Haiti where war and disease got the better of the men. When it was disbanded in July 1797 there were only 349 men and 39 officers left.

Cavalryman in the 1st Regiment.

Cavalryman in the 2nd Regiment.

Hompesh Hussars.

Levied by Baron Hompesh on 27 February 1794, the regiment numbered 350 officers and men; this corps suffered the same fate of the *Rohan Hussars*. It ended up in the Indies where it lost 90% of its strength. The survivors, wounded or ill, were sent back to England. The unit was disbanded in October 1797.

Hussar from *the Béon Legion*.

This legion was levied for Dutch service in March 1793 and was made up of about 140 men. It went over to British service at the beginning of 1795. When the infantry was defeated during the Quiberon affair, the Hussars who had remained in Germany were disbanded towards the middle of 1796.

Equipement and weapons, 'émigrés' Hussars

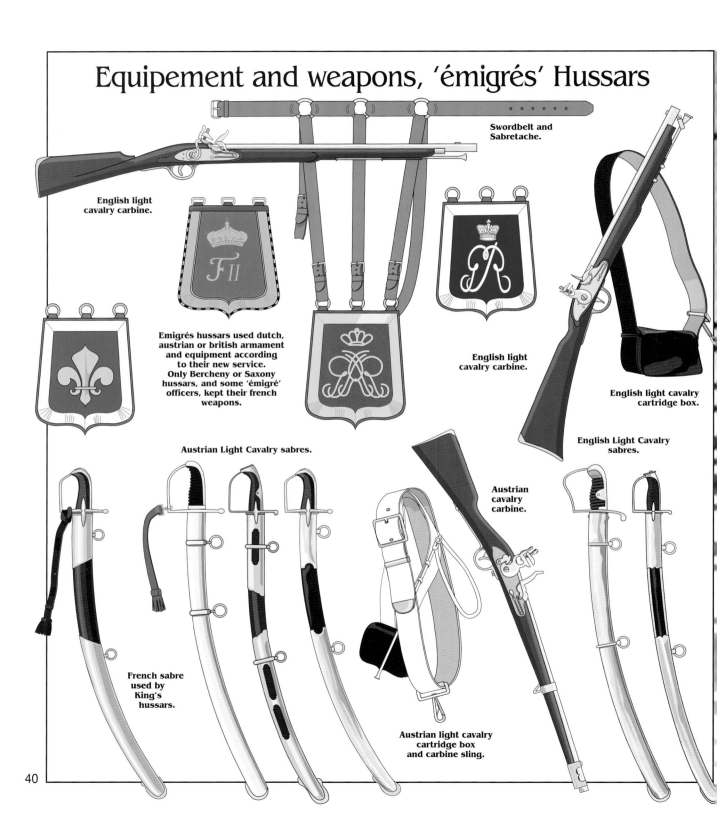

Swordbelt and Sabretache.

English light cavalry carbine.

Emigrés hussars used dutch, austrian or british armament and equipment according to their new service. Only Bercheny or Saxony hussars, and some 'émigré' officers, kept their french weapons.

English light cavalry carbine.

English light cavalry cartridge box.

Austrian Light Cavalry sabres.

English Light Cavalry sabres.

Austrian cavalry carbine.

French sabre used by King's hussars.

Austrian light cavalry cartridge box and carbine sling.

The Hussars 1792-1798

Cavalryman, Trumpeter and officer of the 3rd Hussar Regiment towards 1793-1795.

The cavalryman comes from the set of «*Uniformkünde*» by H. Knötel. The trumpeter is wearing a strange frock coat with lapels and facings drawn by a Dutchman. The officer comes from the 'Méllinet' Collection. He is wearing short boots, a Sub-Lieutenant's trefoil stripe and silvery grey facings instead of the regulation red facings. The hat's cord is the colour of the Republic.

The cavalryman dates from 1792 but his head gear is rather strange for this period when the Ancien Regime was still worn.

The officer was originally drawn by Hoffmann and looks a lot like an officer of the Ancien Regime, even if the shabrack has the initials of the young Republic.

Officer and Cavalryman of the 4th Hussar Regiment.

They are taken from Plate N° 82 of the *French Army* by Lucien Rousselot.

45

The Hussars 1792-1798

Cavalryman in the 4th Hussars during the campaign along the banks of the Rhine, as seen by Kobell, the German artist.

The horse's gear has nothing French about it. The weapons and the equipment come from enemy stores, as and when the regiment needed them. Sometimes the sabretaches don't have their accolades and have rounded ends. Nevertheless the design remained standard and in this case without the Republic's monogram or the number of the regiment.

Cavalryman in the 5th Hussars towards 1793.

According to the Valmont Collection in the Cabinet des Estampes at the Bibliothèque Nationale. He is wearing the riding breeches called 'Charivari'.

From a drawing by Hoffmann, this Colonel in the 6th Hussars like his colleague on the preceding page continues to look rather like an officer of the Ancien Regime.

the Sub-Lieutenant's uniform looks like the one in the 3rd Hussars as far as shape and embroidery go. Mélinet's Collection. Emile Fort Collection. BN

Hussar Officers from the 6th Hussars about 1792-1796.

The Hussars 1792-1798

Officer and Trumpeter in the 7th Hussars during the Helvetian Campaign in 1798.

These uniforms were published in the Passepoil 2nd year after a contemporary drawing by Benjamin Zix. He shows them wearing the French-style coat and the hat in the Hussar regiments.

Cavalryman from the 7th Hussars, towards 1796-1798.

The drawing is taken from the set of engravings by Seele. He shows us a light green dolman, green having been the regiment's distinctive for a short while.

Cavalryman from the 7th Hussars towards 1796-1798.

The 7th was theoretically the only regiment of this period to have grey fur on the pelisse.

Cavalryman from the 7th Bis Hussars towards 1793 with the Army of Italy.

This dress was drawn after the description from documents belonging to the Directeur-General des Habillements (clothing) of the Army of Italy, Poulin, and noted in the E. Fort Collection kept in the Bibliothèque Nationale. As with the 7th, it shows how the hat survived. The sabretache is protected in a sheath made of black waxed cloth.

47

The 8th Hussars 1792-1798

The sabretaches come from the *Musée de l'Armée* et de *l'Empéri* and show some of the variations in their manufacture. One last remark concerning the weapons of these three cavalrymen: none of them has a standard model; German, Austrian sabres were used alongside with the French 1776 model.

Cavalryman in campaign dress about 1799.

He is wearing horse trousers which fasten with a row of buttons down the side seam of the trousers.

Cavalryman wearing campaign dress towards 1799.

Wearing the barrel-sash was not necessarily widespread. Likewise, the leather of the equipment was not always whitened.

Cavalryman according to the set of engravings by Seele.

It shows on the one hand how articles for the harness, even the larger equipment and weapons, were taken from enemy stores and used and on the other hand how, except for the basic colour, the distinctive colour was not always respected. The sabretache is the standard model of the Armies of the Republic; however, an '8' has been embroidered instead of the RF monogram on the left.

Detail of a cavalryman's sabretache (8th Hussars). This model kept in the collections of *the Musée de l'Armée* in Paris.

Detail of a cavalryman's sabretache (8th Hussars). This model kept in the collections of *the Musée de l'Empéri* in Salon de Provence...

The 9th Hussars 1792-1798

Cavalryman of the 9th Hussars
towards 1796.

Shown in the book
on the soldiers of the French
Revolution by L. and F.
Funcken; the German
stamp of the original
drawing can be felt.

Cavalryman of the Hussars
towards 1796.

Unlike the cavalrymen
of the regiment at other times,
this man is wearing a much more
French-style uniform.
The sabretache is a model kept
in the collections of *the Musée
de l'Armée* in Paris.

Trumpeter in the 9th Hussars
towards 1798.

In spite of the principle
of inverting the colours,
the trumpeters in this regiment
adopted a yellow dolman which
they kept until the end
of the Empire.

Cavalryman of the 9th Hussars about 1798.

As with the Hussars in the 4th Regiment, it cannot
be confirmed whether or not all the Hussars
who served in Germany were dressed and equipped
in this manner. It was probably six of one
and a half dozen of the other with the squadrons
equipping themselves as best they could, according
to the circumstances. Drawing from Kobell's series.

The 10th Hussars 1792-1798

Cavalryman in the 10th Hussars.

At the time, there were already dolmans with 5 rows of buttons.

Cavalryman of the 10th Hussars about 1796 after a drawing by J. Domange.

Again there is the German stamp in the saddlecloth and the shabrack. The hat is after a period model. The pennant has a different colour on each side we do know of only pennants with normally one colour on one side and black cloth on the other. The shabrack is the standard model.

Trumpeter of the 10th Hussars.

Drawn after an engraving by Hoffmann, this trumpeter shows that the French hat and coat have been kept in this regiment.

Detail of a cavalryman's sabretache (10th Hussars). This model kept in the collections of *the Musée de l'Armée* in Paris.

This 10th Hussars' sabretache. This model was adopted during the first french Republic.

The Hussars 1792-1798

Cavalryman and Trumpeter from the 11th Hussars towards 1796.

This cavalryman comes from a set of watercolours by Knötel;
His sabretache has a white stripe all round the edges.
The standard bearer of the 11th Hussars on page 53
hoists a sabretache with a tricolour stripe. This item is similar
to the 12th Hussars' sabretache conserved
in the *Musée de l'Armée*'s collections in Paris.
This seems to show that the 12th was not the only regiment
to adopt this type of edging. Was this due to dislike
for the white stripe which had too Royal a connotation?
The trumpeters colours are not inverted
which is not what the regulations stipulated.
The regimental iron-grey would indeed
have given him a very sad colouring...

This 11th Hussars' sabretache.
This model was adopted during
the first french Republic.

Cavalrymen of the 12th
Hussars about 1796.

Coming from the Mountain
Hussars who have been
already presented
in the Chapter about
Volunteer Hussars,
it is possible that when
they converted
to the 12th Hussars,
the brown uniform may have
been used alongside items
from the sky-blue uniform
as these were progressively
changed.

The Hussars 1792-1798

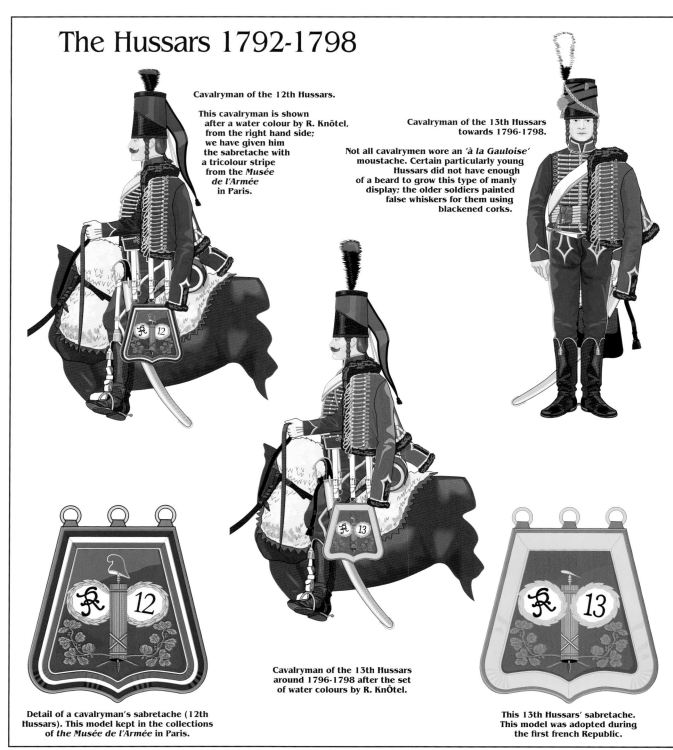

Cavalryman of the 12th Hussars.

This cavalryman is shown
after a water colour by R. Knötel,
from the right hand side;
we have given him
the sabretache with
a tricolour stripe
from the *Musée
de l'Armée*
in Paris.

**Cavalryman of the 13th Hussars
towards 1796-1798.**

Not all cavalrymen wore an *'à la Gauloise'*
moustache. Certain particularly young
Hussars did not have enough
of a beard to grow this type of manly
display; the older soldiers painted
false whiskers for them using
blackened corks.

**Cavalryman of the 13th Hussars
around 1796-1798 after the set
of water colours by R. KnÔtel.**

**Detail of a cavalryman's sabretache (12th
Hussars). This model kept in the collections
of *the Musée de l'Armée* in Paris.**

**This 13th Hussars' sabretache.
This model was adopted during
the first french Republic.**

52

Standards and Guidons

Obverse of one of the 9th Hussars
standards, manufactured
with the 8 number.

9th Hussars Standard.

In a report addressed to the Committee of Public
Safety, Colonel Citizen Levasseur-Dumont,
commanding the Liberty Hussars, expressed the
wish to have his regiment take the eighth place in
the order of the Hussars and at the same time
designed a standard with the number 8.
This report does not seem to have been followed up
though like standards were carried by the 9th
Hussars between 1793 and 1795.

Reverse side
of the 1794-1803 model standard
of the 2nd Squadron.

Guidon of the 1st Squadron, 11th
Hussar Regiment, 1794-1803 model.

It was 36 in by 24 in with a gold and
silver fringe (the tricolour edge
indicated the 1st Squadron). Drawn
by Rigo for his plate N°230 in Le
Plumet, he explained the origins of
the document which enabled him to
make this plate.

Guidon-bearer of the 1st Squadron,
11th Hussar Regiment.

This is a *Maréchal des Logis chef*.
He is equipped with a cartridge case
and musket shoulder-belt which
the NCOs did not normally wear.
Boltrope attached to the guidon's
shaft is hooked to the shoulder-belt
which then serves as holder
for the guidon.

The Distinctives in 1796

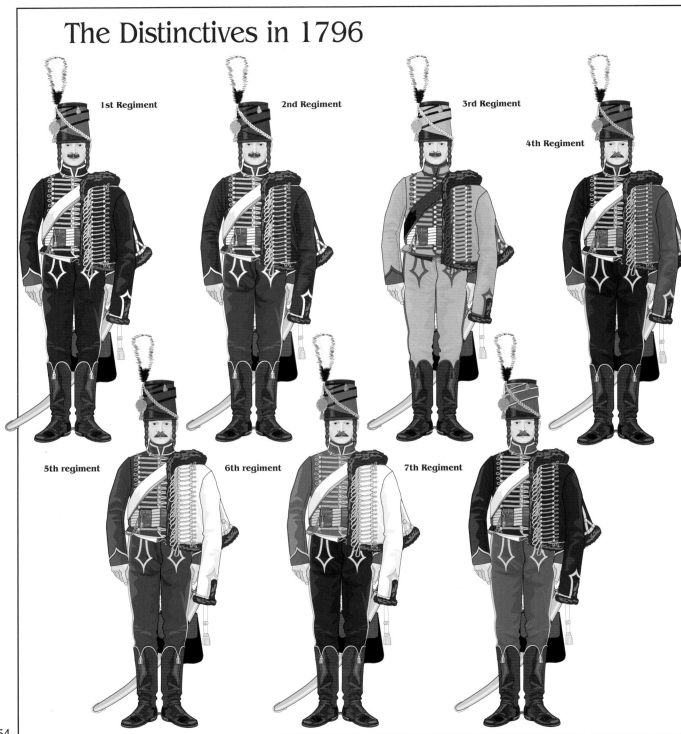

1st Regiment

2nd Regiment

3rd Regiment

4th Regiment

5th regiment

6th regiment

7th Regiment

The Distinctives in 1796

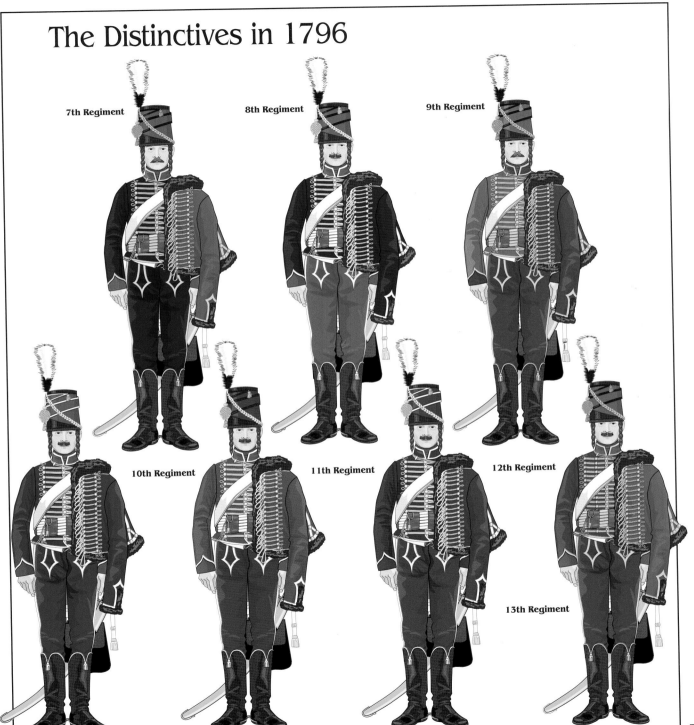

7th Regiment

8th Regiment

9th Regiment

10th Regiment

11th Regiment

12th Regiment

13th Regiment

The 7th Bis Hussar Regiment in Egypt 1798-1801

Cavalryman probably
at the time
of his arrival
in Egypt.

The 7th Bis was the only Hussar regiment to be incorporated into the Expeditionary Corps under the orders of General Bonaparte. They took part in his victories as they did in the defeats after his departure, until they were repatriated to France aboard British ships in 1801.

Cavalryman in full dress
about 1800.

One of the features
of the 7th Bis Regiment
was that they wore
blue breeches in winter
and red breeches
in summer.

Cavalryman wearing campaign
dress towards 1800.

The uniform has been adapted
to the climate and after
the experience of marching
in the desert every horseman had
to carry a metal bottle
or a goatskin of water.
The raw woollen coat was worn
saltire-wise to guard against
sabre-strokes. It was often
replaced by a burnoose.
The sabretache was a curious
model and was noted down
by Rigo in a picture
in the Versailles Museum
and used in an article about
Uniforms in the 7th Bis in Egypt.

Trumpeter wearing
a coat according
to H. Boisselier.

The 7th Bis Hussar Regiment in Egypt 1798-1801

Trumpeter wearing campaign dress, after a watercolour by Lucien Rousselot in the Musée de l'Armée.

Senior Officer according to a study by H. Boisselier on the uniforms of the Expeditionary Corps in Egypt.

Officer wearing campaign dress, after a lithography by Carl Vernet.

Turkish-style equipment has replaced some of the French items, which were less shiny: the saddle has a very high cantle, the saddle tree pistol holsters and the stirrups are most certainly captured. The richness of the Mameluke equipment strongly impressed the French horsemen. Officers and men knew how to take what they wanted in terms of booty. Our officer is armed with a blunderbuss, following the orders of the commanding general, who wanted all cavalry officers to be thus equipped.

Officer wearing full dress around 1800.

The Volunteer Hussar Reserve

Cavalryman in full dress. Considered as being part of an elite unit, the troops wore a red plume.

Cavalryman wearing a pelisse after contemporary drawings by Albrecht Adam in the Army of General Moreau in 1800.

Cavalryman in full dress.

Cavalryman in barrack dress according to A. Adam.

The Volunteer Hussar Reserve or Bonaparte's Hussars were recruited in Paris, Compiègne or Dijon in March 1800. In some ways it was Bonaparte's first attempt to attract the young rich into the ranks of the Army by means of a prestigious uniform. The second and third attempts were the Gendarmes d'Ordonnance and the Gardes d'Honneur. These horsemen very soon to be nicknamed the *'Canary Hussars'*, who equipped themselves and found horses at their own expense. The officers and NCOs were appointed by means of a competition based only on aptitude tests. Unfortunately, recruitment was far from reaching satisfactory numbers and in order to complete their strength, 132 'poor' Hussars were enlisted. The corps fought in Switzerland and with the Army of Germany before being dismissed in April 1801.

Cavalryman wearing summer dress according to Carl Vernet.

The Volunteer Hussar Reserve

Cavalryman in stable
dress. The strips
down the sides
of the breeches
were made
of chamois leather.

Trumpeter wearing a coat.
Wearing the shapska
here is not an isolated
case in the Light Cavalry;
other trumpeters wore
this Polish headdress
which became very
popular during
the Empire.

Cavalryman in town dress.
Note on the collar
the diamond-shaped
patch.

NCO Adjudant in full dress.
He is distinguished
by the three silver stripes
above the dolman's and
the pelisse's facings.
The fur was fox-skin
and he is not wearing
a musket shoulder strap.

The Volunteer Hussar Reserve

Cavalryman in full dress.

Cavalryman wearing full dress according to the drawings of Albrecht Adam.

The condition the drawing is in has not enabled us to make a sufficiently accurate drawing of the sabretache. However, the elements which go to make it up are clear and correspond to the models in use at the time. It was planned to make the shabrack out of bearskin, in all probability sheepskin was used.

Brigadier in full dress.

Faced with supply difficulties, the portmanteau does not correspond to that which was originally planned, iron grey cloth with white and sky blue braid.

The 2nd Hussar Regiment

Cavalrymen from the Centre Company
and the Elite Company created in 1802.

This is from the set of gouaches made
by Colonel Barbier who commanded
the regiment at the time. This first-rate
testimony shows us that the Hussars' uniform
had undergone only slight changes
since the reign of Louis XVI. The headgear
and the sabretache mainly, at least
in the symbols they show.
The harness has not been modified.
The sheep-skin shabrack
which covers the saddle is a smaller model,
but this was not widespread. Armament subsequently
became more disparate, due to the various different types brought out during
the Revolution and the captured arms taken from enemy depots.

The 2nd Hussar Regiment

Trumpeters from an Ordinary Company and an Elite Company.
Taken from the set of gouaches by Colonel Barbier.

They are both wearing inverted colours
for the dolman and the pelisse. The man from
the Elite Company is wearing a special hat called
the 'hairy' shako. It was an ordinary shako covered
with black hairs, but it did not last long.

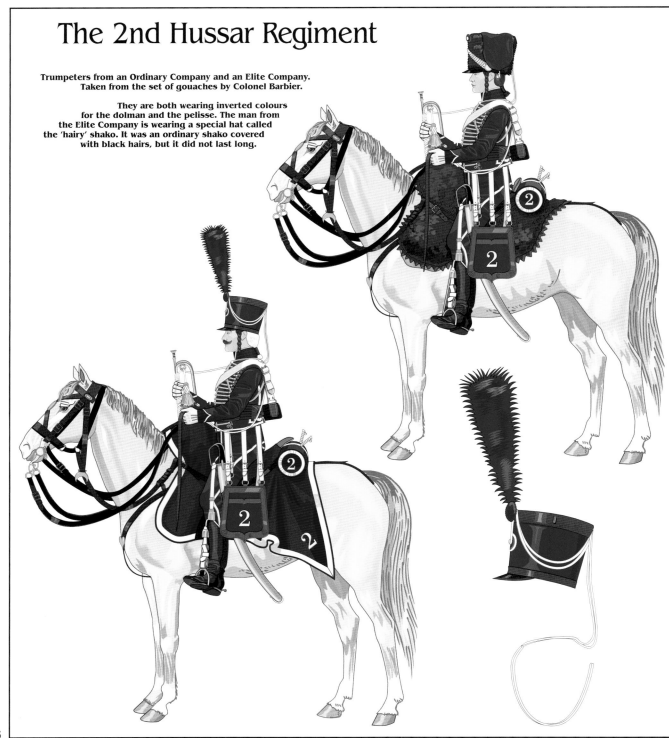

The 2nd Hussar Regiment

Officer wearing a tail coat.

The regiment's officers
in Holland in 1803
are shown
with a sky
blue shabrack.

Officer wearing a frock coat.

This item of clothing for officers
was already described
in the 1786 Regulations.
The sabretache was the officer's model
without the fringes,
or the trooper's model
with the number '2'
embroidered in silver.

Senior Officer in full dress.

As with a lot of officers he is not
wearing a lovelock.

Senior officer
on the regimental staff.

The 2nd Hussar Regiment

Colonel Barbier, officer commanding the 2nd Hussars.

This is rather a self-portrait of him with his staff, whose dress has been reproduced in the previous pages. The picture is not detailed enough to show the shape of the harness buckles or the type of sabre he was carrying and which we have had to interpret. However, bridles, breast strap and crupper were made of red leather, decorated with studs and other motifs, the same colour as the buttons.

Cavalryman wearing service dress towards 1800.

Cavalryman in town dress about 1800.

The shako's pennant is worn with the blue side on the inside.

The 3rd Hussars Regiment

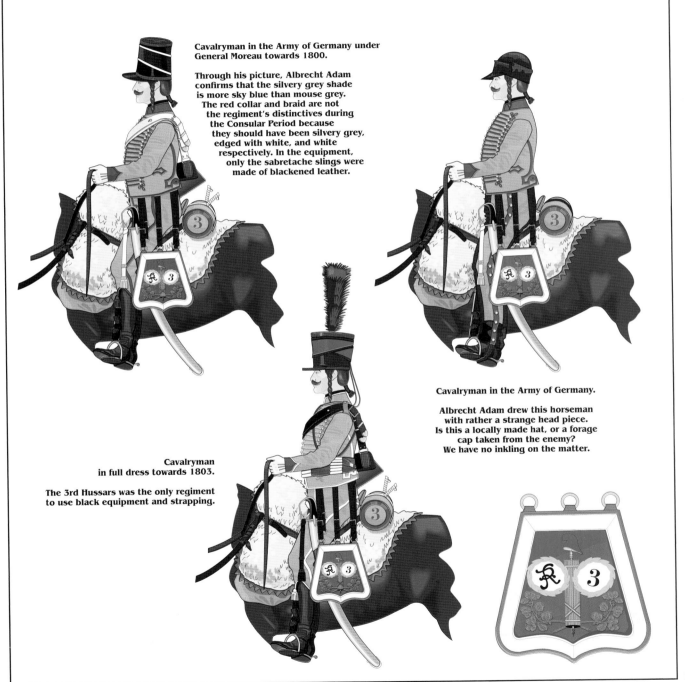

Cavalryman in the Army of Germany under General Moreau towards 1800.

Through his picture, Albrecht Adam confirms that the silvery grey shade is more sky blue than mouse grey. The red collar and braid are not the regiment's distinctives during the Consular Period because they should have been silvery grey, edged with white, and white respectively. In the equipment, only the sabretache slings were made of blackened leather.

Cavalryman in the Army of Germany.

Albrecht Adam drew this horseman with rather a strange head piece. Is this a locally made hat, or a forage cap taken from the enemy? We have no inkling on the matter.

Cavalryman in full dress towards 1803.

The 3rd Hussars was the only regiment to use black equipment and strapping.

The 4th Hussar Regiment

Cavalryman with the Army of Germany towards 1800.

He is wearing the hat with the detachable visor with its pennant showing the coloured side.

Cavalryman in campaign dress about 1800.

Thanks to all the different representations, we have noticed that uniforms can vary within the same regimen

Cavalryman in campaign dress towards 1800.

It was A. Adam who saw this horseman with blackened leather equipment.

Cavalryman in full dress, circa 1803

Trumpeter in campaign dress with the Army of Germany towards 1800.

This drawing by A. Adam confirms the inverted colour for the dolman still in use at the beginning of the Empire. This is not an elite company as these were only created in 1802.

The Hussars during the Consular Period

Cavalryman from
an Ordinary Company
of the 5th Regiment
about 1803.

Cavalryman from the Elite
Company of the 5th Regiment.

The Elite Companies were created
in 1802 and were distinguished
by the colback bearing a scarlet
plume and decorated
with a pennant
of the same colour.

Trumpeter
of an ordinary company
of the 5th Regiment
towards 1803.

Colonel of the 6th Hussars.
This is Brigade Commander
(Colonel) Pajol.

As shown by Rigo
in his plate, he is wearing
a rather curious visor-less
shako decorated with
interlacing golden rings.
The aglet shown on the front
of the helmet is positioned
here in the middle.
He is wearing an all gold-
coloured barrel-sash.

The Hussars during the Consular Period

Cavalryman from the 7th Bis Regiment.

The distinctive colours do not correspond to those we have given in the Chapter devoted to the 7th Bis in Egypt. The colours of the dolman and the pelisses are the other way round.

Cavalrymen from the 8th regiment.

This sabretache preserve its revolutionary decorations.

Maréchal des Logis in off duty dress.

Cavalryman of the 7th Regiment.

The sabretaches shown here date from the Consular Period. The first (top) is in the Musée de l'Empéri. It was probably only issued to the 1st Squadron. The second appears in several sources and the third dates back rather to the end of the Consular Period, or even to the beginning of the Empire; it also had a dark green background.

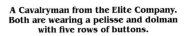

A Cavalryman from the Elite Company. Both are wearing a pelisse and dolman with five rows of buttons.

The Hussars during the Consular Period

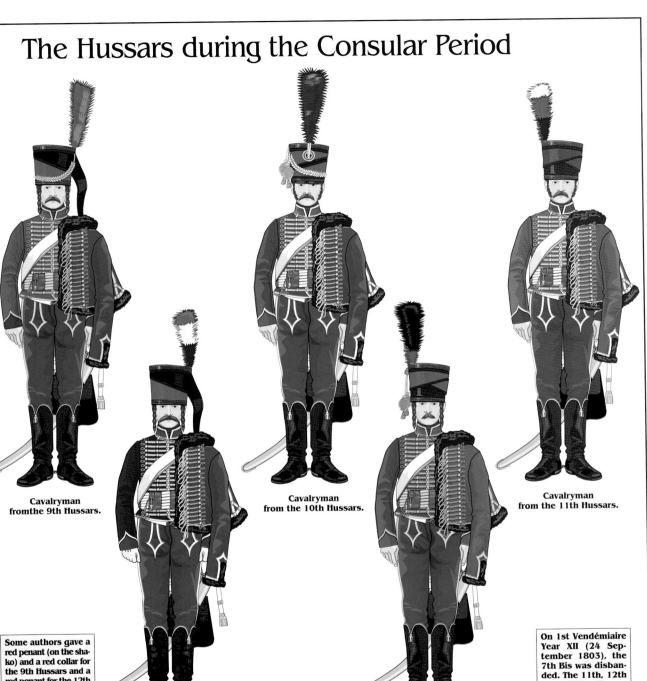

Cavalryman from the 9th Hussars.

Cavalryman from the 10th Hussars.

Cavalryman from the 11th Hussars.

Cavalryman from the 12th Hussars.

Cavalryman from the 13th Hussars.

Some authors gave a red penant (on the shako) and a red collar for the 9th Hussars and a red penant for the 12th Hussar regiment. According to the regulation table, these components might be sky blue.

On 1st Vendémiaire Year XII (24 September 1803), the 7th Bis was disbanded. The 11th, 12th and 13th Hussar regiments were transferred to the Dragoons in 1803.

The Distinctives as at 24 September 1803

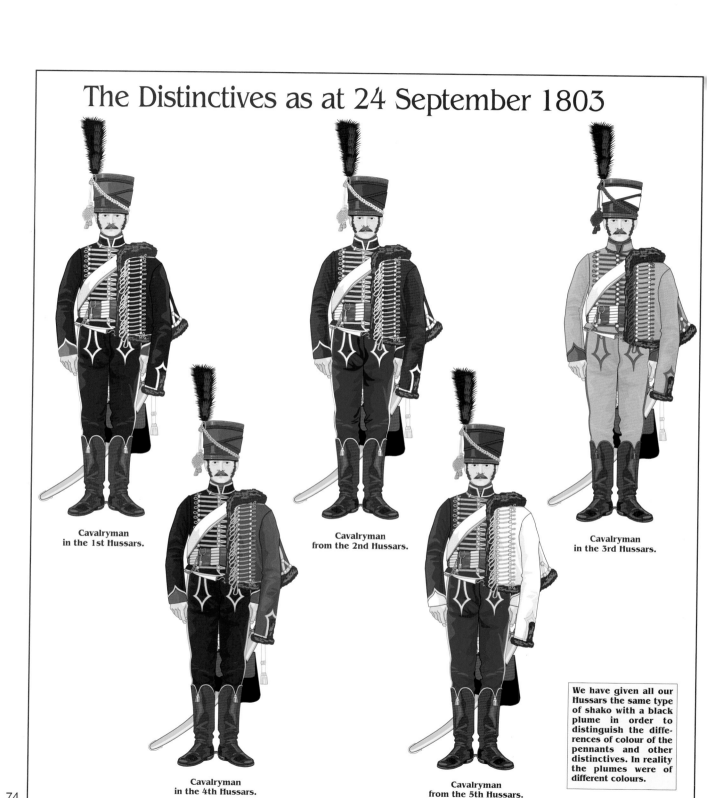

Cavalryman
in the 1st Hussars.

Cavalryman
from the 2nd Hussars.

Cavalryman
in the 3rd Hussars.

Cavalryman
in the 4th Hussars.

Cavalryman
from the 5th Hussars.

We have given all our
Hussars the same type
of shako with a black
plume in order to
distinguish the diffe-
rences of colour of the
pennants and other
distinctives. In reality
the plumes were of
different colours.

The Distinctives as at 24 September 1803

Cavalryman
in the 6th Hussars.

Cavalryman
from the 7th Hussars.

Cavalryman
in the 8th Hussars.

Cavalryman
in the 9th Hussars.

Cavalryman
from the 10th Hussars.

THEN IT WAS THE EMPIRE

The second volume of this study will show the uniforms worn by the Emperor's Hussars between 1804 and 1815 in detail. Let us now give a short portrait of the light cavalryman who went all over Europe for ten years jostling

the enemy squares, scouting for the Grande Armée, capturing towns, writing a legend for this French type of Light Cavalry for more than a century.

The period began with ten regiments and ended with fourteen. The distinctive colours were fixed for these first ten units from 1803 and did not change until the end of the Empire.

The Hussar during the Empire

The Hussar who fought in 1805 under Napoleon was not very different from the one who obeyed the directives of the First Consul, Bonaparte. The silhouette of the Light Cavalryman changed very slowly between 1804 and the 1812 Regulations.

The pelisse and the dolman were shortened again towards 1808 and 1809 only. If the dolman could

now be worn fully closed, the same cannot be said for the pelisse because of the thickness of the fur around the edges. Only the first braids could be fastened.

Under the pelisse, the Hussar could not wear the dolman, but only a plain or braided (according to the regulations for each regiment) waistcoat. The dolman was worn alone or with the pelisse over the shoulder.

The Hungarian-style breeches did not change, but were eventually replaced by the tan-coloured horse trousers called the 'charivari'.

The boots were shorter than during the preceding period. They were cut, heart-shaped, bordered with Russian braid and decorated with a cloth tassel; the black sheepskin and the leather tassel were also visible. The spurs were now rivetted to the heel and no longer fastened to the stiffener.

The shako was bigger and was given a pair of metal-scale chinstraps. The plate was not necessarily adopted by all the regiments.

	1st Hussars	2nd Hussars	3rd Hussars	4th Hussars	5th Hussars	6th Hussars	7th Hussars	8th Hussars	9th Hussars	10th Hussars
PELISSE										
Background cloth	Dark Sky blue	Brown	Silvery grey	Scarlet	White	Blue	Dark green	Dark green	Sky blue	Sky blue
Sheepskin Linning	White	White	White	Blanc	White	White	White	White	White	White
Sheepskin edging	Black	Black	Black	Black	Black	Black	Black	Black	Black	Black
Braid	White	White	Scarlet	Yellow	Lemon yell.	Yellow	Bright Yellow	White	Yellow	White
Buttons	White	White	White	Yellow	Yellow	Yellow	Yellow	White	Yellow	White
DOLMAN										
Background cloth	Dark Sky blue	Brown	Silvery grey	Half royal blue	Sky blue	Scarlet	Dark green	Dark green	Scarlet	Sky blue
Collar	Dark Sky blue	Brown	Silvery grey	Half royal blue	Sky blue	Scarlet	Scarlet	Scarlet	Sky blue	Scarlet
Facings	Scarlet	Sky blue	Scarlet	Scarlet	White	Scarlet	Scarlet	Scarlet	Sky blue	Scarlet
Braid	White	White	Scarlet	Yellow	Lemon yell.	Yellow	Bright Yellow	White	Yellow	White
Buttons	White	White	White	Yellow	Yellow	Yellow	Yellow	White	Yellow	White
WAISTCOAT	Scarlet	Sky blue	Silvery grey	White	Sky blue	Scarlet	Scarlet	Scarlet	Sky blue	Scarlet
BREECHES	Dark Sky blue	Sky blue	Silvery grey	Half royal blue	Sky blue	Scarlet	Scarlet	Scarlet	Sky blue	Scarlet
BARREL SHASH										
Cord	Crimson	Crimson	Crimson	Crimson	Crimson	Crimson	Crimson	Crimson	Crimson	Crimson
Barrel	White	White	White	Yellow	Lemon yell.	Yellow	Bright Yellow	White	Yellow	White
SHAKO										
Body	Black	Black	Black	Black	Sky blue	Scarlet	Black	Black	Black	Black
Base of the plume	Black	Black	Black	Black	Black	Red	Black	Black	Black	Black
Top of the plume	Black	Sky blue	Black	Black	Red	Black	Black	Red	Yellow	Red
Cord and tassel	White	White	Scarlet	Yellow	Lemon yell.	Yellow	Bright Yellow	White	Yellow	White
Metal part of the chinstrap	White	White	White	Yellow	Yellow	Yellow	Yellow	White	Yellow	White

The 1st Hussar regiment, 1804-1806

Cavalryman wearing full dress.

Cavalryman wearing training dress (stable jacket).

Cavalryman in full dress in 1804 according to the set of drawings by Hoffmann.

Cavalryman from the Centre Company in barracks dress. Note the scarlet waistcoat.

Cavalryman from the Elite Company wearing off duty dress.

The sabretache has lost its republican attributes and now only displays the number of the regiment.

The 1st Hussar regiment, 1804-1806

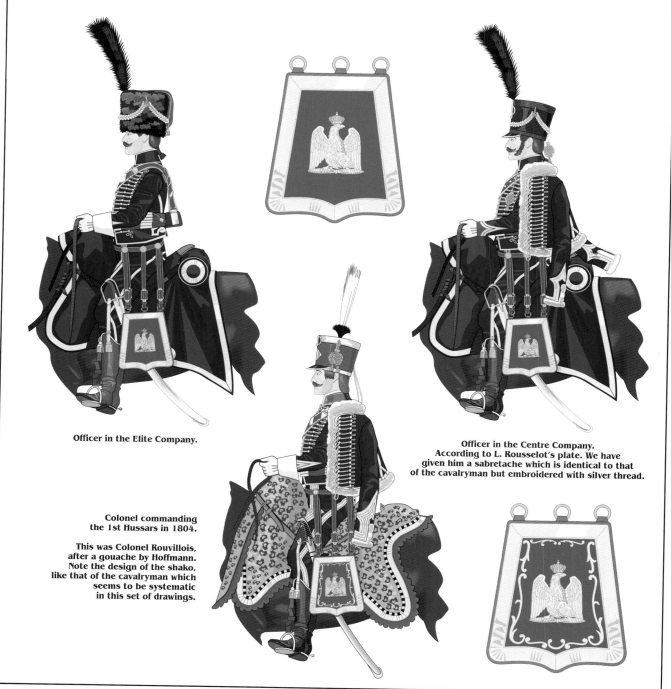

Officer in the Elite Company.

**Officer in the Centre Company.
According to L. Rousselot's plate. We have
given him a sabretache which is identical to that
of the cavalryman but embroidered with silver thread.**

**Colonel commanding
the 1st Hussars in 1804.**

**This was Colonel Rouvillois,
after a gouache by Hoffmann.
Note the design of the shako,
like that of the cavalryman which
seems to be systematic
in this set of drawings.**

The 2nd Hussar regiment, 1804-1806

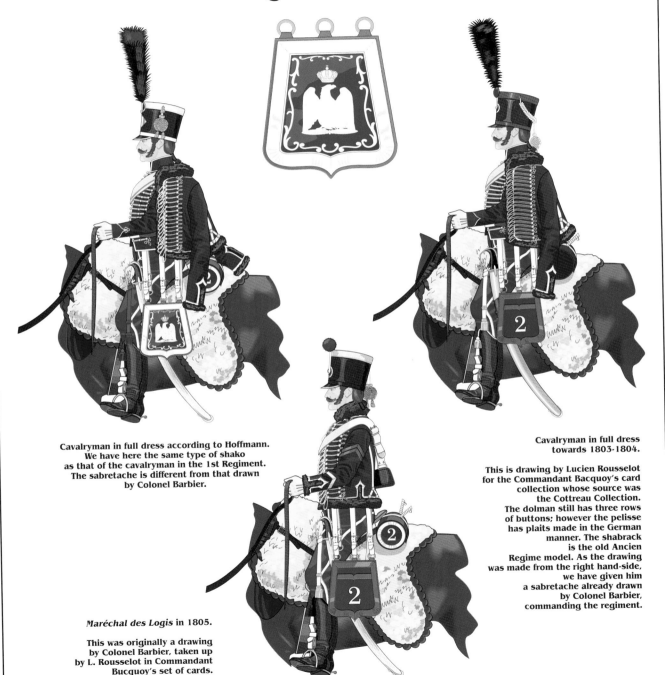

Cavalryman in full dress according to Hoffmann.
We have here the same type of shako
as that of the cavalryman in the 1st Regiment.
The sabretache is different from that drawn
by Colonel Barbier.

Maréchal des Logis in 1805.

This was originally a drawing
by Colonel Barbier, taken up
by L. Rousselot in Commandant
Bucquoy's set of cards.

Cavalryman in full dress
towards 1803-1804.

This is drawing by Lucien Rousselot
for the Commandant Bacquoy's card
collection whose source was
the Cottreau Collection.
The dolman still has three rows
of buttons; however the pelisse
has plaits made in the German
manner. The shabrack
is the old Ancien
Regime model. As the drawing
was made from the right hand-side,
we have given him
a sabretache already drawn
by Colonel Barbier,
commanding the regiment.

HARNESS GLOSSARY

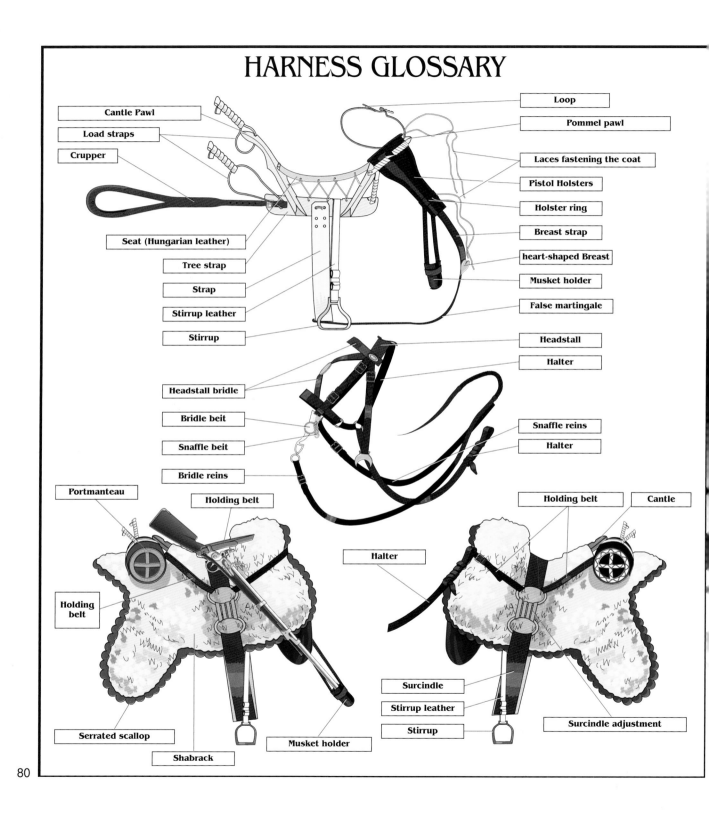

Cantle Pawl

Load straps

Crupper

Seat (Hungarian leather)

Tree strap

Strap

Stirrup leather

Stirrup

Loop

Pommel pawl

Laces fastening the coat

Pistol Holsters

Holster ring

Breast strap

heart-shaped Breast

Musket holder

False martingale

Headstall bridle

Bridle beit

Snaffle beit

Bridle reins

Headstall

Halter

Snaffle reins

Halter

Portmanteau

Holding belt

Holding belt

Cantle

Halter

Holding belt

Surcindle

Stirrup leather

Stirrup

Surcindle adjustment

Serrated scallop

Shabrack

Musket holder

UNIFORM GLOSSARY

Plume

Cockade braid

Cockade

Flounder

"Cadenettes"

Tie

Ball buttons

Braid

Dolman

Sash

Tassel

Pointed facings

Hungarian knot

Hungarian-style Breeches

Gland

Hungarian-style boots

Shako cord

Tassel

Scale chinstrap

Chinstrap rosette

Collar

Pelisse collar

Pelisse

Cartridge case shoulder-belt

Musket shoulder-belt

Sabre suspension hook

Barrel sash

Light Cavalry sabre

Sword-knot

Sabretache

Sabretache pocket

Riding breeches

Riveted spurs

Shako top

Flounder Cord

Pennant

Shako body

"Bourdalou"

Flounders

Tail

Coat

Cartridge-case

Water bottle

Musket

Basane

Decoration or number

BIBLIOGRAPHY

Uniformes de l'Armée française de Lucien Rousselot
— Hussards généralités, 1790-1804. Planche n° 9.
— Les hussards de Lauzun. Planche n° 12.
— Les hussards du règlement de 1786. Planche n° 51.
— Le 4e Hussards, 1789-1815. Planche n° 82.

Planches Le Plumet de Rigo
— Hussards 1er régiment. Planche U1.
— Hussards 2e régiment. Planche U4.
— Hussards 3e régiment. Planche U10.
— Hussards 5e régiment. Planche U13.
— Hussards à pied. Planche U15.
— Hussards 6e régiment. Planche U18.
— Hussards 7e régiment. Planche U21.
— Hussards 8e régiment. Planche U24.
— Hussards volontaires de la réserve. Planche U27.
— Hussards trompette du 5e. Planche n° 185.
— Les hussards de 1770-1789. Planche n° 16. E. Lelièpvre.
— Planches uniformologiques de J. Domange.

Books
— La cavalerie française et son harnachement.
Colonel Dugué Mac Carthy. *Edition Maloine.*
— Guide à l'usage des costumiers et artistes. H. Malibran.
— Histoire de la cavalerie française. Général Suzanne.
— Les troupes émigrées, vicomte de Grouvel, édition à compte d'auteur.
— Recueil de Valmont.
— La cavalerie au temps des chevaux.
Colonel Dugué Mac Carthy, *EPA*
— Les équipements militaires 1600-1870. Tome II.
M. Pétard, *édition de l'auteur.*

— L'armée pendant la Révolution.
G. Lediberder, *Collection historique du Musée de l'Armée.*
— Les soldats de la Révolution Française
L. et F. Funcken, *Castermann.*
— La cavalerie légère. Cdt. Bucquoy. *Editions Jacques Grancher.*
— Emigré and foreign troops in british service
R. Chartrand, P. Courcelle, *Men at arms n° 328, Osprey*
— Napoleonic uniforms, J. Elting, *Mac Millan*

Magazines
— Cavalier d'autrefois. P. Begnini, *Passepoil n° 2.*
— Les volontaires étrangers de la Marine. D. Peyrot, *Bulletin du CFFH 81/04*
— *Carnet de la Sabretache* spécial Hussards, année 1970.
— Les hussards de la République. Rigo, *Uniformes n° 33.*
— Les extraordinaires tenues de l'Armée d'Orient. Rigo, *Uniformes n° 76.*
— Les hussards de Choiseul. Patrice Courcelle, *Uniformes n° 94.*
— Les hussards de Lauzun. Michel Pétard, *Uniformes n° 96.*
— Les hussards du premier Consul. Rigo, *Tradition n° 66/67.*
— Les régiments de hussards pendant la Révolution.
G. Jaeger, *Tradition n° 155.*
— Le 10e Hussards. J. Domange, *Tradition n° 151.*
— Les hussards à la veille de la République. M. Pétard, *Figurines n° 39.*

Archives
— Collection du Musée de l'Armée, Paris.
— Collections du Musée de Nancy.
— Collection « *Vivat Hussard* ». Musée des hussards de Tarbes.
— Archives historiques de l'Armée de Terre, Vincennes,
cotes : XC249 à 261XC209 et 217XC223 à 230
— Cabinet des Estampes de la Bibliothèque Nationale,
collection Emile Fort.

ACKNOWLEDGEMENT

We would like to thank *Rigo, Michel Pétard, Dr François-Guy Hourtoulle, M. Lapray* and *Jean-Louis Viau* for their precious help as much morale-wise as editorially.
We would like to pay them the tribute which they deserve.

Design, creation, lay-out and realisation by ANDRE JOUINEAU and JEAN-MARIE MONGIN.
Re-reading and updating DENIS GANDILHON and JEAN-LOUIS VIAU. © *Histoire & Collections* 2004
Computer Drawings by André JOUINEAU

SA au capital de 182 938,82 €

5, avenue de la République
F-75541 Paris Cédex 11
Téléphone : 01 40 21 18 20
Fax : 01 47 00 51 11

This book has been designed, typed, laid-out and processed by *Histoire & Collections*, fully on integrated computer equipment

Printed by ECGI
Spain, European Union

OFFICERS and SOLDIERS

Available

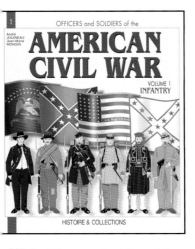

N° 1. *Officers and soldiers of the*
American Civil War
Volume 1
Infantry

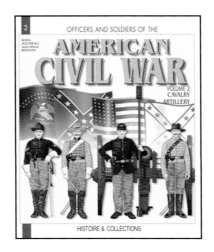

N° 2. *Officers and soldiers of the*
American Civil War
Volume 2
Cavalry, artillery

N° 3. *Officers and soldiers of the*
French Imperial Guard, 1804-15
Volume 1
Foot soldiers

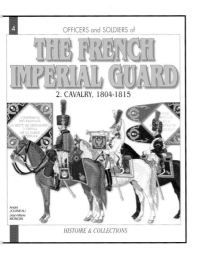

N° 4. *Officers and soldiers of the*
French Imperial Guard, 1804-15
Volume 2. Cavalry

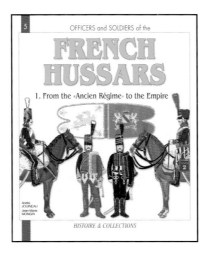

N° 5. *Officers and soldiers of the*
French Hussars, 1786-1815
Volume 1

Coming soon

N° 6. *Officers and soldiers of the*
French Hussars, 1786-1815
Volume 2

OFFICERS and SOLDIERS. FRENCH HUSSARS, 1786-1815

Volume 1. FROM THE ANCIEN REGIME TO THE EMPIRE, 1786-1804

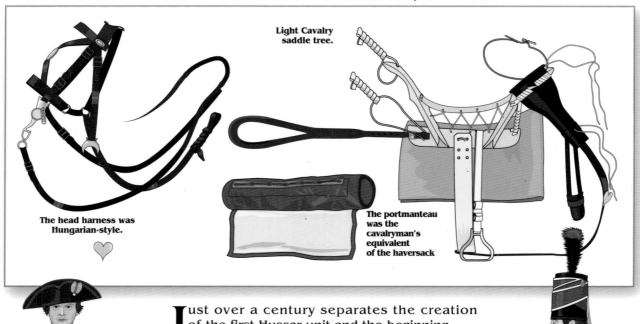

Light Cavalry saddle tree.

The head harness was Hungarian-style.

The portmanteau was the cavalryman's equivalent of the haversack

Just over a century separates the creation of the first Hussar unit and the beginning of this study.

The first royal Hussars regiment was formed in Strasburg in 1693, after the good behaviour of *'these Hungarian deserters'* whom the Maréchal of Luxemburg used to give the rear of the enemy troops a hard time. Disbanded in 1697, the regiment was reformed four years later. It was offered by the Elector of Bavaria to Louis XIV and took the name of *Saint-Genies Hussars* in 1707,

On 1 October 1786, new regulations were brought out concerning uniforms, equipment and weapons for the King of France's Armies.

To a greater or lesser degree, these regulations — in many ways they were almost legendary — set the standard for soldiers' uniforms to come until the middle of the First Empire.

ISBN : 2-915 239-03-7

9 782915 239034

Histoire & Collections
5, avenue de la République
F-75541 Paris Cédex 11

Tél. : 01 40 21 18 20 — Fax :
01 47 00 51 11

OFFICERS and SOLDIERS of the

FRENCH HUSSARS

2. From the 1st to the 8th Regiment 1804-1812

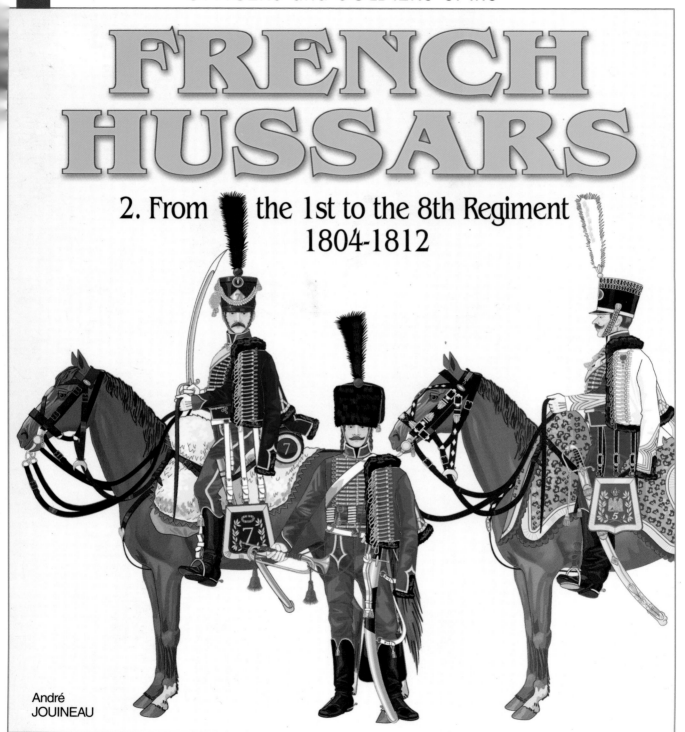

André
JOUINEAU

HISTOIRE & COLLECTIONS